DAVID HARE

The Judas Kiss

faber and faber
LONDON · BOSTON

First published in 1998
by Faber and Faber Limited
3 Queen Square London WC1N 3AU

Typeset by Faber and Faber Ltd
Printed in England by Mackays of Chatham plc, Chatham, Kent

© David Hare, 1998

A CIP record for this book
is available from the British Library

ISBN 0-571-19431-1

2 4 6 8 10 9 7 5 3 1

Pour mon amour

The Background to the Play

In 1895, the Marquess of Queensberry, enraged by rumours of his son Lord Alfred Douglas's relationship with the Irish playwright Oscar Wilde, entered Wilde's club and left him a note accusing him of 'posing as a sodomite'. When Wilde decided that he could not ignore the challenge, and that he must bring a prosecution against Queensberry for criminal libel, the Marquess retaliated by searching London for a list of young men willing to testify against Wilde. Knowing of this list, Wilde nevertheless persisted with his case. After his private suit collapsed in two days, Wilde himself became liable for public prosecution under Section 11 of the Criminal Law Amendment Act of 1886, which had made 'acts of gross indecency' between men a criminal offence.

On 19 May 1897, Wilde was released after two years in jail. He went abroad at once and never returned to England before his death in 1900.

Characters

Oscar Wilde
Lord Alfred Douglas
Robert Ross
Arthur Wellesley
Phoebe Cane
Sandy Moffatt
Galileo Masconi

Act One: Deciding to Stay is set in London in 1895.
Scene One: Lunchtime.
Scene Two: Teatime.

Act Two: Deciding to Leave is set in Italy in 1897.
Scene One: Dusk.
Scene Two: Dawn.

The Judas Kiss was first presented by the Almeida Theatre Company, in association with Robert Fox and Scott Rudin, at the Playhouse Theatre, London, on 12 March 1998. The cast was as follows:

Oscar Wilde Liam Neeson
Lord Alfred Douglas Tom Hollander
Robert Ross Peter Capaldi
Arthur Wellesley Alex Walkinshaw
Phoebe Cane Stina Nielsen
Sandy Moffatt Richard Clarke
Galileo Masconi Daniel Serafini-Sauli

Director Richard Eyre
Designer Bob Crowley
Lighting Mark Henderson
Music George Fenton
Sound John A. Leonard

Some say a cavalry corps
some infantry, some, again,
will maintain that the swift oars

of our fleet are the finest
sight on dark earth; but I say
that whatever one loves, is.
                    Sappho

Every man contains his own death as the fruit
contains the stone.
                    Rilke

Act One: Deciding to Stay

SCENE ONE. *Friday 5 April 1895. Romantic orchestral music. A streak of light falls near a bed on which a young couple are making love in a curtained room. The bed is in considerable disorder, a riot of counterpanes, blankets, sheets, and materials in rich brocade. The young woman, Phoebe, is 17, milk-white and beautiful. The young man, Arthur, is only a little older, short, sturdy, blond and handsome. In the shadows, she is seen dimly to climb away from him, his face pressed deep into her as she rises. Standing on the bed, Phoebe is now spreadeagled, her arms against the wall in a gesture of crucifixion, as Arthur kneels against her. The stage picture is Renaissance: abandoned white flesh against rich patterns, passion expressed as religious torment.*

The light spreads. The outline of an ornate hotel room becomes clearer. To the left of the bed, a huge window is swagged in rich material. To the right, a door. As their excitement grows, a discreet knocking begins. It goes unremarked. The knocking becomes louder. Arthur's name is called urgently. Then louder. Finally Phoebe hears it. Then Arthur hears it too. The music fades.

Phoebe Oh Lord God Almighty.

Like a frightened animal, she pulls free and runs across to the bathroom. Arthur holds a sheet against himself as he goes to unlock the door. He opens it a crack to check, then opens it further. Mr Moffatt is a refined, feline Scot in his 50s, wearing tails.

Moffatt Ah, Arthur, I thought it was you.

Arthur Mr Moffatt.

Moffatt You will forgive me if I let in some light.

Moffatt has come into the room and is heading to the window. Arthur has closed the door, but seems unperturbed. Like Phoebe, he is quite strongly cockney.

Arthur You'll see, sir. I haven't yet started . . .

Moffatt has drawn the curtain. Light floods from the window on to the floor. The scene is of late-night abandon. Draperies strewn over the room, flowers, bottles, old meals uncleared from tables.

Moffatt My goodness. You have had some reckless enjoyment, I see.

Arthur Hardly, Mr Moffatt. This wasn't our doing. We were just about to start clearing it up.

Moffatt I would hope. Who was helping you?

Arthur Oh, the new maid.

Moffatt Where is she?

Arthur She's in the bathroom.

Moffatt I see.

Arthur Her name's Phoebe.

Moffatt Thank you. I am apprised of her name.

Arthur She's settling in nicely.

Moffatt Yes, Arthur. I think I had worked that out for myself. (*He seems untroubled by the scene.*) Does she want to come out of the bathroom?

Arthur I think she may want to, sir.

Moffatt (*raising his voice*) Phoebe, do you want to come out?

Phoebe (*from the bathroom*) I need my clothes, sir.

Moffatt Very well. I shall turn my face to the wall.

Moffatt stands facing the wall. Phoebe comes out of the bathroom, still naked. Arthur helps her as she searches, unamused.

What are you doing?

Phoebe I'm looking for my smaller garments, sir.

Arthur holds up a pair of knickers.

Arthur Here.

Phoebe Thank you.

Moffatt If you avail yourself of the bathroom, we can make headway in here.

Phoebe Thank you, sir.

She goes out to the bathroom. Moffatt turns. Arthur has had a sheet round him, but now he lets it drop. He stands naked. Neither man moves.

Arthur I'd not thought Lord Alfred would need his room quite so quickly.

Moffatt Let us do this work together. Together we shall do it in no time at all.

After a moment Moffatt moves across the room to start work. Arthur goes to pull his undergarments on.

Arthur Lord Alfred doesn't normally get back till the evening.

Moffatt That may explain your behaviour. It hardly excuses it.

Arthur No, sir.

Moffatt Lord Alfred has had to make a sudden change in his plans.

Arthur Oh, I see.

Moffatt Hence the urgency. (*He lifts various silver lids on a side-table.*) Last night's champagne, by the look of it. The remains of a lobster. Plainly he has no respect for crustaceans. This looks like Chef's *moules marinières.*

Arthur, naked to the waist, goes to help Moffatt stripping the bed.

Did you visit any other rooms this morning?

Arthur Oh yes, sir. I've cleared out the dishes from most of this floor.

Moffatt Alone?

Arthur Phoebe was helping me.

Moffatt Really? And did you christen each room?

They work on at the bedclothes. Phoebe comes back, adjusting her maid's uniform.

Do you think you could get me the baskets?

Phoebe I'll get them.

Moffatt Ah, Phoebe, yes, right.

Phoebe goes, intending to open the main door.

And also . . .

Phoebe Yes, sir?

Moffatt Could you ask your friend Arthur to put on the rest of his clothes?

Arthur smiles and moves towards his abandoned

4

clothes. Phoebe goes into the corridor.

Arthur, I shall need to speak to you later. You have indulged in behaviour the hotel cannot possibly condone. I shall need to reprimand you in person.

Arthur Yes, sir.

Moffatt That's clear?

Arthur goes on dressing.

Arthur When do you wish this act of discipline to take place?

Moffatt After work. When exactly do you get off?

Arthur Five-thirty.

Moffatt Right, after.

Arthur Yes, sir.

Moffatt I'll wait for you outside the kitchens.

Arthur The kitchens it is, sir.

Phoebe comes back with a basket for the dirty laundry.

Moffatt The hotel has standards it must maintain.

Robert Ross has appeared at the door. He is a short man, not yet 30, with a puck face, Buster Keatonish, and beautifully dressed. He is in obvious distress.

Ah, good morning, Mr Ross.

Ross Good morning.

Arthur is now dressed. He and Phoebe bow and bob to Ross.

Arthur and Phoebe Morning, sir.

Moffatt Lord Alfred's room is not quite ready, I fear.

Ross I'm afraid there's some luggage.

Moffatt Of course, sir. Arthur.

Arthur goes out to get it, leaving the door open.

Ross I am expecting Lord Alfred presently. My fear is our presence is already known.

Moffatt Sir?

Ross I came through the lobby. Has someone been talking?

Moffatt Impossible.

Ross I'm grateful.

Moffatt It is out of the question. The Cadogan is a steadfastly private hotel.

Phoebe goes out again with dirty sheets.

Ross That is its reputation. That was the purpose in choosing it. You know why we came here.

Moffatt Indeed, sir.

Ross Lord Alfred needed somewhere discreet.

Moffatt Discretion is something we pride ourselves on.

Arthur appears smartly with a big bag.

Arthur The bag, sir.

Ross Please, just put it down where you will.

Arthur If it's Lord Alfred's, sir, then I'll unpack it.

Ross No. It isn't Lord Alfred's.

Moffatt now smoothly intervenes.

Moffatt That's fine, sir. We quite understand.

Phoebe reappears urgently at the door.

Phoebe Sir, there are people . . .

Moffatt What people?

Phoebe Somehow they've got up the stairs.

Ross turns away in panic.

Ross It starts! It starts even now!

Phoebe They do look like journalists.

Ross Oh Lord, this is just as I feared.

Moffatt I apologize, sir. Have no concern, sir. You will not be inconvenienced, you have my assurance.

Ross Thank you. We must have some moments of absolute calm.

Moffatt Of course, sir. They will be provided. No question. Excuse me.

Ross Thank you.

Phoebe Back in a tick.

Moffatt has gone. Phoebe follows. Arthur opens new sheets for the bed. Moffatt can be heard admonishing the journalists outside, 'Gentlemen, gentlemen . . .' Ross looks uncomfortably across to Arthur.

Ross I'm sorry. It's our fault. We caused all this upset.

Arthur Sir?

Ross Last night a group of us ate in this room.

Arthur It's fine, sir.

Ross I'm afraid we only parted at five.

Arthur Did you have an enjoyable evening?

Ross No, I could not say enjoyable. Why no, not at all.

Arthur continues his work, the soul of politeness.

Arthur I've noticed Lord Alfred is addicted to company. He rarely likes to be on his own.

Ross No. No, he is companionable.

Arthur Yes, sir. That's what I meant. Since he came here – what is it? – five weeks ago, I've seen him with a whole range of companions.

Ross Yes. Yes, Lord Alfred is always sociable.

Arthur Indeed, sir. It would be a dull world without company. Are you fond of company yourself?

Ross I? (*He looks at Arthur thoughtfully a moment.*) Oh yes. Within moderation. Sometimes. Occasionally. But always at my own choice.

At once, Lord Alfred Douglas ('Bosie') arrives, followed by Moffatt. He is a startlingly handsome young aristocrat, 23, fair-haired and volatile.

Bosie It is simply absurd, it is unendurable . . .

Moffatt (*bowing*) Lord Alfred . . .

Ross Bosie, you must calm down.

Bosie I cannot believe what has happened.

Ross I know.

Bosie Even now I cannot believe it.

Ross Where is Oscar?

Bosie He is on his way here.

Ross What are you saying? Do you mean you have left him?

8

Bosie I could not endure that solicitor!

Ross Oscar is travelling alone?

Bosie I simply got up and walked out. (*He turns, anticipating Ross.*) It's all right, Oscar and I had already decided. It was better we travelled apart. Somebody spat at us. It is known throughout London that our case has collapsed. The crowds all yell at us. They shout out abuse. The indignity is beyond all description. To have our names in their mouths! (*He turns to Moffatt.*) I need a glass of cold water. Get it!

Moffatt Yes, sir.

Bosie From a bottle! A bottle! None of that filthy sewage that flows from your taps.

Moffatt turns to Arthur who has been working on, quietly ironic.

Moffatt A bottle of water for Lord Alfred.

Arthur At once, sir.

Bosie Why is this room in such vile disarray?

Arthur goes out. Phoebe joins Moffatt to continue tidying up.

Ross Oscar has finished the letter?

Bosie Yes. It is written.

Ross Is it dispatched?

Bosie To the *Evening News*. Saying the reason he was forced to abandon his case is he could not allow me into the witness box. He had to protect me!

Ross He is making that clear?

Bosie is shaking his head in anger.

Bosie He would not allow me to dispute with my father in public. It drives me to distraction.

Ross I know.

Bosie I, who was better placed to denounce my own father than anyone! And yet it is Oscar who forbids me to advance my own cause.

Ross is uneasy of this talk in front of the staff.

Ross He has explained to you. It would not be advantageous . . .

Bosie Not advantageous?

Ross He thought it would do you no good.

Bosie looks at him wildly, as if he's mad.

Bosie Oh well, how brilliant! What a brilliant decision! And how exactly could things have worked out worse than they have? This disgusting little man, this vandal, who has pretty well ruined my life. And I am not allowed to speak of his appalling behaviour! And why not? Oh, because it is not Oscar's wish . . . (*He turns, addressing the whole room.*) And the result? It hardly needs saying: the case is in ruins. The two of us face equal disgrace. He made this fatal mistake. He did not call me!

Ross No. (*He looks round, wanting to get rid of the staff.*) Just one minute . . .

Bosie And now – very well – through his own stubbornness, *now* he is paying the price!

Ross Yes. If you could allow us one moment . . . is it Phoebe?

Phoebe is carrying Bosie's books across the room.

Bosie Leave those things there! Just leave them! I asked for some water.

Phoebe Yes. (*She stands, taken aback by his outburst.*)

Ross I apologize. Lord Alfred is under great strain.

Bosie Robbie, you always speak for me. In everything. Even with the servants, you speak as if I were not in the room. Always I am not allowed to speak! From this habit of silencing, from the way you have all made me silent, from this our present predicament stems.

Arthur comes back with a silver tray.

Well, I'll be silent no longer!

Arthur Your water, sir.

Bosie What?

Arthur The water you asked for. It's here.

Bosie frowns as if not understanding.

Bosie So? Set it down. Come on, what are you expecting? Tribute? What are you waiting for? Praise?

Arthur No, sir. Do you want me to pour it?

Bosie Pour?

Arthur Do you want me to pour it, sir?

Bosie Yes, of course. Do it, Arthur. What is the alternative? It pours itself? Hardly. Mr Moffatt, this staff you employ! Where do you find them? The music-hall? Robbie, do you have some money? Will you give young Arthur here a penny or two?

Ross Yes, of course.

Bosie I'll repay you. (*Bosie's mood has changed, so he is almost skittish to Moffatt.*) What are they, music-hall comics?

Moffatt You told me before, sir, you'd been very happy

with everything the staff had done for you here.

Bosie is already bored and wanders away. Ross tips Arthur and Moffatt.

Bosie Yes, oh yes. If you say so.

Ross Mr Moffatt, thank you. Here's something for you.

Moffatt The room is not yet ready, I fear.

Ross As long as you guarantee us security, we shall truly require nothing else.

Moffatt has opened Wilde's case on the bed. Phoebe bobs insolently, and they are all gone. The room is roughly restored to order.

Bosie, you realize I do have to speak to you.

Bosie I know you must speak to me. You have adopted your headmaster's tone. 'Come into my study'!

Ross Only because what I must say is important. We have little time. It is vital. (*He pauses.*) You know I have been to his house.

Bosie Yes.

Ross I have picked up his luggage.

Bosie Have you?

Ross At his instructions, I have also cashed him a cheque. Protest all you like, you know what is happening. He is set on a path. A path he is now determined to take. (*He is holding up Wilde's pocketbook.*) He will come here only briefly. It is essential. He must not stay long.

Bosie No, of course not.

Ross waits. Bosie shouts resentfully.

Of course not!

Ross He needs to keep moving.

Bosie looks at Ross, decisive.

Bosie No, first, I suggest he must stop and take stock.

Ross No!

Bosie Robbie, the truth is he has never thought this thing through. He has never examined it! He took up the challenge without giving it the care it deserved. And now it has collapsed . . .

Ross Yes.

Bosie He still has not realized! He has not yet grasped that it is all his own fault!

Ross stays quiet, patient.

Ross Bosie, that is no longer what matters . . .

Bosie Yesterday, making that joke in the courtroom – even you must see that did him no good . . .

Ross Plainly.

Bosie That says it all! This need to perform!

Ross Yes. But just at this moment, it's scarcely important.

But Bosie is ignoring him.

Bosie Finally, that instinct is lethal. When asked of an Oxford college servant if he had kissed him: 'Oh no, I did not kiss him. He was far too ugly.' In front of the jury!

Ross I know . . .

Bosie It was not a good joke. Not even a good joke! There was no reason except to show off.

Ross No.

Bosie I had warned him. Yet from the moment he said it . . .

Ross I know. I know. You have said this.

Bosie From the moment he said it, our case was finished. We abandoned all chance of victory.

Ross I know. All of us said all this last night.

But Bosie takes no notice.

Bosie I had said to him, I had told him one thousand times, 'Be modest.' I said, 'I am English, you are not.' The English people do not like wit. They abhor those who are cleverer than they are. But he did not listen. No. (*He suddenly raises his voice again.*) Robbie, he has not listened throughout!

Ross No.

Bosie If he had taken my advice from the beginning. But his friends were against me. They advised him not even to respond to the original affront . . .

Ross Well . . .

Bosie They counselled against litigation. His friends all said there was no need to fight! (*He turns to Ross as if Ross had spoken.*) Oh really? Then do what? Stand condemned as a coward? Let my father insult him in the world's eyes? No. He had to fight! He had to. But this is the heart of the matter! He's been badly advised throughout this whole business.

Ross That is as may be.

Bosie It's as I tell you.

Ross Perhaps. But just at this moment, it is hardly the point. (*He tries to be precise to gain Bosie's attention.*) Your father's solicitors have passed on the papers. We know this. We've been told this for sure. They were dispatched to the Attorney-General over two hours ago.

Ross has tried to calm him, but Bosie seems to miss the point.

Bosie Oh, Robbie, come on, why do you think I sent for my cousin? This is exactly what I foresaw!

Ross steps towards him, still quiet.

Ross Bosie, in a moment Oscar will come here. We will only have a short time. In conditions of calm and absolute seriousness, he will have to settle his resolve on the path he must take.

Bosie Of course.

Ross The Attorney-General is even now speaking to the Home Secretary. It is assuredly only a matter of time. Asquith will give his consent. Pretty soon the local magistrate will issue his warrant for Oscar's arrest. (*He puts up a hand.*) Yes. You heard us this morning with Oscar's solicitors. If we stop and examine the evidence, if we look at that list – that disastrous list of young men – well, is it wise . . . is it truly courageous to stay here? Fight on when he has no chance to win?

Bosie Who says?

Ross Listen. Or rather, is it simply foolhardy? In open court, these men will bear witness. They will say the most terrible things. Things no one will ever forget. Whether he wins or he loses, Oscar's reputation will be destroyed for all time.

Bosie You say that.

Ross Very well.

Bosie I deny it.

Ross You may well deny it. That is your right. But your denial is not of the essence. Nothing now matters save Oscar's own view.

There is a silence. Bosie looks cannily at Ross.

Oscar has looked into the abyss. He has seen all the dangers. He will now leave the country. Yes. That is his decision. To leave it for ever. And you must respect this choice he has made.

They both look, neither man relenting.

By his nature, we both know Oscar can be excited. How do I say this? He can be swayed. I recognize this truth about Oscar. He is always available to your point of view. I am not seeking to silence you. Be assured. You may say what you like. I ask you, simply take care. There must be no hysteria. You may argue, but you must not dictate. This is the point I am making. On this occasion, because his whole future depends on it, I beg you, let Oscar set his own course. I know I can trust you, Bosie. Behave in a way which gives Oscar a chance.

The room is silent. But Bosie seems more amused than sobered.

Bosie Oh, Robbie, you always speak prettily.

Ross Thank you.

Bosie Considerate. Modest, as always. Well-tempered. Does it never occur to you? Life has handed you the easiest role.

Ross What role?

Bosie Third party. Robbie, anyone can play third party. It requires no real talent. You play it to perfection, but bear this in mind: it is a role of no consequence. That's him!

He moves across the room because Mr Moffatt can be heard in the corridor beckoning Wilde to follow him.

The role can be taken by anyone at all.

*Oscar Wilde comes through the door. He is just over 40
with long hair, not at all the languid pansy of legend.
He is solid, tall and fleshy, 6'3", a mixture of ungainli-
ness and elegance. Mr Moffatt is behind him, carrying
two small bags.*

Moffatt In here, sir, please, come in, the others are waiting . . .

Bosie Oh, Oscar.

Ross Oscar, you're here.

Wilde What is this? Oh, Bosie, dear Bosie . . .

Bosie Oscar . . .

They fall into each others' arms, hugging.

Wilde Bosie . . .

Bosie Oscar, oh, Oscar . . .

Ross and Moffatt stand quietly waiting.

Wilde Forgive us, Mr Moffatt, Lord Alfred and I have
been parted for almost an hour.

Moffatt I quite understand, sir.

Wilde We have survived the shock of separation. The
strain has been awful. On my side at least. And journalists now seem to be holding some sort of professional
convention in your lobby. Mr Moffatt has kindly guided
me through.

*Arthur has arrived with an ice bucket and bottles on a
tray.*

Arthur Wine, sir.

Wilde Robbie, can you give Mr Moffatt some money?

Ross Why, yes, of course.

Wilde Please put my bags on the bed. Thank you.

Ross Oscar, remember, you do not have long.

Ross tips Moffatt, who puts the three bags together on the bed.

Bosie Robbie is desperate that nothing should detain you.

Ross Bosie . . .

Bosie He's given me a lecture on how I am to behave.

Wilde Oh, Robbie, that was superfluous. Bosie at all times behaves impeccably.

Ross I have not said otherwise. Oscar, just tell us, what is your news?

Wilde My news?

Ross Yes.

Wilde My news? I have none. Everyone hourly awaits my arrest. They seem astonished that I am still at liberty. But, my friends, all I can say is: by a miracle, I have achieved the Cadogan.

Moffatt Indeed, sir.

Wilde In spite of everything, I am finally here. And surrounded by friends, I would say, Mr Moffatt . . .

Moffatt I would hope, sir . . .

Wilde And Arthur. Good Arthur. The excellent Arthur as well. Oh Lord . . . (*He grips Arthur's hand tightly.*)

Moffatt Come, you must sit, sir . . .

Wilde No, no, I am steady. I am here but I cannot yet say for how long. (*He moves to hide his tears, then animates himself to keep cheerful.*) It appears that the whole of

London is fleeing. People had told me, now I see for myself. I looked from my coach. I saw every invert in the metropolitan area packing his bags and heading for France.

Ross looks nervously to the staff.

It is a veritable mass migration. I'd never imagined diaspora could be on this scale.

Ross Well . . .

Wilde The takings at certain fashionable restaurants will tonight be counted in pennies. At a single stroke opera will be stone dead as a form.

Ross (*nervously*) Yes.

Wilde I was astonished at who appeared on the streets. There is scarcely a *métier* which is not represented. All of the rabbits are being smoked from their holes. (*He turns and sees his bags on the bed.*) What remain of my worldly possessions. You had them sent over?

Ross Yes. As we agreed, I went to your house.

Wilde Thank you. Thank you, dear Robbie.

He moves over and hugs Ross, then looks into his eyes. Ross speaks quietly.

Ross Please bear in mind, Oscar, you do not have long.

Moffatt Excuse me, do you also want coffee, sir? Have you eaten?

Wilde Have I eaten? Oh Lord, let me think.

Ross Oscar, I'm afraid it's out of the question. You simply do not have time.

Wilde Do I not?

Ross You are here to say your goodbyes to Bosie. Also, I needed you to pick up your things.

Wilde Yes, of course. But a small drink, please, Robbie, you must not deny me . . .

Ross Why, no.

Wilde And then, of course, I shall get going. I shall go on the instant.

Arthur Do you want to taste, sir?

Wilde Pour away. Hock tastes like hock, and seltzer like seltzer. Taste is not in the bottle. It resides in one's mood. So today no doubt hock will taste like burnt ashes. Today I will drink my own death.

He lights the first of many cigarettes. Ross has turned to Moffatt.

Ross Mr Moffatt, on my orders a cab is waiting downstairs . . .

Moffatt Yes, sir.

Phoebe has appeared at the door by chance, bringing towels.

Ah, Phoebe, will you please tell the driver outside that Mr Wilde . . .

Ross His passenger, do not call him Mr Wilde . . .

Moffatt His passenger is here and will be down very soon.

Phoebe Yes, I see, sir.

Ross You have that message?

Phoebe Yes, of course. The passenger who is not Mr Wilde is coming and the message is he will not be long.

She glares at him resentfully, then goes. Arthur hands Wilde the wine.

Wilde Thank you, Arthur.

Bosie looks up, quietly confident.

Bosie I would like to talk to you, Oscar.

Wilde Talk to me? Bosie, truly! You hardly need ask.

Bosie No?

Wilde Of course not. Come, talk.

Bosie I had an impression from Robbie.

Wilde What impression? (*He looks between them.*)

Bosie Robbie implied that your wish was that I should step back.

Wilde (*frowns*) Did you, Robbie? Did you say that?

Ross Not at all. Not entirely.

Wilde Then what did you say?

Bosie is enjoying Ross's discomfort.

Ross I was saying . . . I was saying only that you yourself need to make haste.

Bosie Oscar, even now my cousin is having meetings at the Houses of Parliament to make sure this prosecution need never take place.

Ross Bosie, it's simply impractical. I have no doubt your cousin is doing his best. But there is a train. If Oscar delays, if he does not catch it, then he loses everything.

Bosie Yes, and if he does take it, he wakes up tomorrow . . . Yes! Is that what you want? His life spent then in some foreign country? What's worse, the real possibility he will never get back?

Both of them have begun to raise their voices. Wilde smiles, calm.

Wilde Please, the two of you, I must impose myself. Robbie, what time is it?

Ross It is just past two-thirty.

Wilde And, tell me, what time is the train?

Ross hesitates a second.

Tell me the time the actual train leaves.

Ross The train leaves at four.

Wilde Ah, well then . . .

Ross It connects with the boat.

Wilde The Cadogan to Victoria, let us be realistic. In the name of our common humanity, let us get our priorities straight. Let us pause, let us make the seminal decision: it seems that I still have time for my lunch.

Satisfied, he turns to Moffatt. Ross shifts, furious.

Moffatt Sir.

Wilde Be fair to me, Robbie. I face a long journey. I dread *mal de mer*. I shall need to travel with some ballast inside. (*He turns again to Moffatt.*) Mr Moffatt, I need something suitable. Perhaps a small lobster. Seafood, certainly. *A l'Americaine*. With some kind of rice.

Moffatt Chef does a rice which is perfumed.

Wilde Or a timbale. Exquisite. Perfect for crossing the Channel. (*He turns to Bosie.*) Bosie, be quick now. What would you like?

Bosie Nothing. I couldn't. When even now my father is gloating, standing like some mad animal on the steps of the court, screaming that if ever I am seen in your company, then he will have you shot like a dog.

Wilde smiles absently at him and turns back to Moffatt.

Wilde And langoustines I suppose are quite simply unavailable?

Moffatt My regrets. But the season.

Wilde Don't worry. I quite understand.

Ross is still tense.

Ross Very well. It is your decision. I would only remind you the press now know where you are.

Wilde That is clear.

Ross If you stay in this room, I do have to warn you, at any moment the police may appear.

Wilde That will give my lunch an added spice of excitement.

He turns back to Moffatt, who is about to leave. Phoebe has returned with towels.

Oh, Mr Moffatt, I wonder, with lobster do I really want rice?

Ross Oscar . . .

Moffatt We offer excellent dauphinoise potatoes.

Wilde Do you recall if I have eaten those before?

Moffatt Yes, sir.

Wilde And were they not heavy? Are they not more suitably a dinner-time dish?

Ross All right, eat all you like. Just as long as you are quick. But there are things I must tell you. I have to remind you I have been to your house.

The atmosphere is changed at once. Wilde looks thoughtfully at Ross. Moffatt, alert to the mood, bows tactfully.

Moffatt We shall go, sir. I shall bring you both dishes. The rice and the potatoes. Then you can choose.

Wilde Excellent, Mr Moffatt. And thank you, Arthur, as well.

Arthur Not at all, sir.

Wilde Phoebe. Is it Phoebe?

Phoebe It is.

The three find themselves lined up opposite Wilde for an oddly formal moment.

Wilde Throughout this time of trial I've had excellent service. Whenever I've visited, I have been made to feel welcome. It's something which means a great deal to me. No, truly. Thank you. I'm moved by it.

Moffatt Our pleasure, sir.

Wilde is once more on the edge of tears.

Wilde Robbie, a cue for more money.

Ross Oscar, that is not what this money is for!

Wilde You know I can't abide meanness.

Ross Very well. I shall give them some of my own.

Wilde This is in character. Robbie is a true Christian.

Ross Here. (*He reaches into his pocket for coins.*)

Moffatt, Phoebe and Arthur Thank you. Thank you very much, sir. Greatly appreciated.

Ross Now, I'm sorry, but we really do need to be on our own.

Moffatt, Arthur and Phoebe go out. Wilde has gone across to put a glass in Bosie's hand.

Wilde Will you have some wine with me, Bosie? Look, there is more than one glass. Here. Please. Stay close to me, Bosie. I need you. You and I still have a long way to go.

Wilde kisses Bosie on the cheek. There is a silence. Then Wilde moves away.

Ross I have to report to you. I have seen Constance.

Wilde You saw her?

Ross Yes.

Wilde And what did she say? Tell me, how were the children?

Ross I did not see them. But she assured me the children were well.

Wilde Go on.

Ross She is in the most terrible turmoil. There is only one way to relieve it. She asked me to beg you: she implores you to flee.

There is a moment's silence. Bosie watches from the side.

Look . . .

Wilde You say you caught no sight of the children?

Ross No. My impression was they were playing in the nursery.

25

Wilde I see. And do they . . . do they yet have any knowledge of what has happened?

Ross Constance says they know nothing at all. (*He waits a moment.*) For their sake, she says, you must choose exile. If you stay and battle it out at a trial, the prospect of what will be said, what will be repeated in London . . . well, their lives will not be worth living. She is sending them abroad.

Wilde looks up.

Tomorrow.

Wilde She is sending the children?

There is a silence. For the first time Wilde seems deeply hurt.

I see.

Ross Flight is imperative for the whole family. She was relieved when I gave her your news.

Wilde My news?

Ross Yes.

Wilde You said I had already decided?

Ross I described our meeting last night.

Wilde Did you say who was there?

Ross To be truthful, I mentioned the others. But I did not mention Lord Alfred. Understand, I did not think it was fair. (*He pauses a second, tactful.*) You must realize . . .

Wilde Oh, I do . . .

Ross She has conceived a most passionate resentment. To say at this point that . . . that you still meet with Bosie, that you take account of his views . . .

Bosie interrupts, furious.

Bosie Oh really, I cannot endure this!

Ross Why not?

Bosie This whole thing makes no sense at all!

Ross Why?

Bosie Because we did not decide! We have not decided! My recollection is quite firm on this point. Exile was only one choice among many.

He looks to Wilde, who looks into his glass and takes another draught.

This is what we must all decide upon now.

Ross Oh, Bosie, now really . . .

Bosie I mean it. I thought that is what this meeting is for.

Ross Whatever we said, whatever we argued, it is no longer relevant. Look at the reality! Outside a cab will be waiting. It's waiting! I ordered it.

Bosie So?

Ross It will take him to the station. He can do no other. This is the last boat tonight! Oscar?

Wilde reaches again for the wine.

Wilde Do not distress yourself. The hour is fixed in my memory. I know exactly how soon I must go.

And Bosie is already continuing.

Bosie Oscar cannot leave until he hears from my cousin.

Ross Oh really!

Bosie He will come here by three at the latest, he said. He will bring us firm news from Asquith. (*He turns angrily to*

Ross.) Why are you always so scornful?

Ross Because we all know it is going to be simply too late!

Bosie George Wyndham is a man of considerable influence. He is a Member of Parliament. It is madness for Oscar to run headlong from the country until we know beyond any question that a prosecution cannot be stopped.

Ross It cannot be stopped!

Bosie smiles, confident.

Bosie You know nothing. Robbie, forgive me, but the thinking of better-class people is hardly what one might call a strong point of yours. George is a friend of the Prime Minister.

Ross So?

Bosie Robbie, please trust me. I understand these things rather better than you. My name is good for something, I hope. There is not much point in being born with the name of Queensberry unless there are moments when it can be used.

Wilde is quietly amused.

Wilde I wish I shared your faith in the English. Nation to them is just as important as class. They have united at last in hatred of the foreigner. Yes, because I am Irish.

Bosie That's absurd.

Wilde Is it? Yesterday I looked across the courtroom. It shocked me. I tell you, their excitement was more than merely professional. Yes? Did you see that?

Ross nods.

This was a court which ached for a kill.

Ross Yes.

Wilde The whole nation is ready. I have been tolerated for too long a time. No one has rights in this country. One is granted only a temporary licence. And here comes the moment when mine is withdrawn. (*But he is already bored with his own theory and has got up to examine the open case on the bed. He takes out some books.*) What is this? Did you pack these for me?

Ross Certainly.

Wilde *The Thoughts of St Ignatius.* Robbie . . . (*He looks at him reproachfully.*) My God. What is this? This only gets worse. Dickens! Robbie, do you not know me?

Ross I was rushed.

Wilde You think I should gorge myself on sentimental morality?

Ross Very well then, tell me, what would you prefer?

Wilde Why, tales of suffering and murder. Injustice. The spilling of blood. Let my reading be only of ravaging, destruction and rape. That is what I want. Nothing else. And for these things the only book worth considering is the Bible. The essential companion to exile. I shall read it continually.

Ross I shall get you a Bible.

But Bosie is quietly furious.

Bosie Oh, Oscar, please, you do not convince.

Wilde Not convince?

Bosie You're affecting indifference . . .

Wilde Affecting it?

Bosie You are standing there talking about the books you will take.

Wilde A critical discussion of literature seems to me at all times worth having.

Bosie Oh yes? I am not for one second fooled!

Wilde You're not fooled? Why should I be seeking to fool you? You of all people, Bosie. I promise you, nothing in the world could be further from my mind.

Bosie Oh, come on, you know what I'm saying . . .

Wilde Do I? Oh really? Remind me: what do I know?

Bosie If you flee from this country, then it is an evident disaster . . .

Wilde Why, yes. That is clear to me.

Bosie It will mean that my father has won!

Wilde smiles, amused by Bosie's obsession.

Wilde Ah, well then . . .

Bosie He cannot win!

Wilde Of course not . . .

Bosie The man is a monster! He betrayed my mother! He brought his fat mistress into our house! He installed her inside our house . . .

Wilde Indeed.

Bosie It was an open provocation. It is essential he is not seen to succeed!

Wilde shrugs slightly, as if there's nothing he can do, and drinks more.

What's more, if you flee, it's like admitting you're guilty . . .

Wilde Oh yes . . .

Bosie You'll be as good as admitting your enemies were right all along.

Wilde I fear so.

Bosie What, and that does not disturb you?

Wilde Not at this very moment, why no.

Bosie The thought of it? The shame? Being taken for a coward?

Wilde interrupts, smiling.

Wilde Bosie, you say I'm acting indifference. I promise you, I have no need to simulate. My indifference is real.

Bosie Oh, Oscar . . .

Wilde You urge me to take some decision. You say I must now decide my whole fate. Why? To what purpose? If I flee, as you say, it's disastrous. But if I stay, my prospects are also not good. So why make a choice? What are you asking exactly? Why at this moment do anything at all? (*He sits back, confident.*) I have always had a low opinion of what is called action. Action is something my mother brought me up to distrust. Why make a decision which does not yet need to be made? What's more, think of this: I am where I wish to be. Yes. Just at this moment. At least for the instant, things could hardly be better. Consider. I find myself here with you in this room. Yes. With this wine. Where I have been happiest. These past five weeks. The three of us, planning our hopeless campaign.

He smiles affectionately at Bosie. Both Ross and Bosie are silenced.

Outside this room, I will find only suffering. The world is charged. It is poised. My destiny will all too quickly unfold. But while we are here – perhaps you think this shortsighted, but you cannot deny it – the fact is that things are not really too bad.

This is no sooner out than Arthur has knocked on the door, wheeling in a trolley.

Arthur Excuse me . . .

Wilde Ah, food, yes, delicious.

Bosie I'm sorry . . .

Wilde Ah yes, please enter . . .

Bosie Oh, Oscar, you're not really planning to eat?

Wilde Yes, I am.

Bosie How? I mean, *why*? At this moment?

Wilde Yes, Arthur, please do set the table down there. (*He has faltered getting up. He has almost finished the bottle.*) Whoops . . .

Ross Oh God, Oscar, you're stumbling . . .

Wilde No, no. I need a steadying drink. Dear Arthur, some more wine when you're ready . . .

Arthur Yes, sir. (*He has pulled out a folding table and is laying it with a white tablecloth.*) I'm afraid to have to tell you, sir, there's now quite a crowd in the street.

Wilde A crowd?

Arthur Yes. They look like a lynch-mob.

Wilde Indeed?

Arthur They're baying for blood.

Wilde That is quite a coincidence. It has also been wildly exciting in here. The temperature's rising. We live in a ver-itable cauldron of fear. More wine! And shall we nail up the entrance? (*He looks round rather grandly.*) This all confirms me in my decision to stay in this room.

Ross shifts, uneasy.

Ross Oscar . . .

Wilde No, Robbie, please, desist for a second. Allow me this gap. This equipoise. Let me have that. I have perhaps half an hour. Allow me this one sweet moment of peace.

Moffatt appears now at the door.

Moffatt Excuse me, sir. A Mr George Wyndham . . .

Bosie Ah, George . . .

Moffatt He asks if he may be allowed to come in.

Bosie Tell him yes.

Wilde If you don't mind, Bosie, I would prefer it if you saw him outside. No, really.

Bosie Why?

Wilde I can tell he'll be breathless.

Bosie Oh, Oscar . . .

Wilde It's the breathlessness I cannot face.

Bosie Are you going to be childish?

Wilde He'll rush in, wearing those awful striped trousers and bursting with news which he'll want to blurt out. The very name Wyndham! It exudes self-importance. A person called Wyndham indeed! George Wyndham! One can sense him warming the back of his legs by the fire, and discussing the movement of shares.

Bosie is nodding as if this confirms a familiar pattern.

Bosie Oh, I see, so you're going to be facetious. Is that it? Is that how you're going to behave?

Wilde Not at all.

Bosie He may bring you news of your freedom!

Wilde Then, please, by all means you may see him out there in the corridor. I have said. You are welcome to meet him . . .

Moffatt What shall I say, sir?

Wilde I just don't much fancy the prospect myself. (*He is standing, self-consciously capricious, looking for more wine.*)

Bosie Oscar, George has been working . . .

Wilde I know this . . .

Bosie He has been in Parliament all morning on your behalf.

Wilde Tell him I appreciate all he has done for me but I do not wish to speak to him now.

Bosie Why not?

Wilde Because it is simple! Open that door and the real world comes into this room.

Wilde has raised his voice. Moffatt retires discreetly.

Bosie You know this has been the whole story . . .

Wilde What story?

Bosie This has been my problem throughout . . .

Wilde (*to Arthur*) The wine! Can you get me the wine?

Arthur Yes, of course, sir.

Arthur has gone out past Moffatt, who is still waiting, ignored.

34

Bosie It is as if you still can't absorb it. George Wyndham is a powerful man!

Wilde I know that.

Bosie He is my cousin, for God's sake! He has far better things to do with his time.

Wilde I'm sure. (*He smiles surreptitiously at Ross.*)

Bosie For him there is also the danger.

Wilde I see that.

Bosie A man of his standing. The risk he is taking by speaking on your behalf. And why do you think he is doing it? My cousin George is actually risking his neck! Because by the purest coincidence he happens to hate my father almost as much as I do myself!

Wilde looks at him a moment.

Wilde Why, yes.

Bosie So then why will you not talk to him?

Wilde Oh, Bosie . . .

Bosie I mean it! Why won't you? He is waiting outside!

Wilde Oh, Bosie, how I envy your spirit! (*He stops, the point reached at last.*) I do not wish to speak to George Wyndham because the point is George Wyndham cannot succeed! (*He seizes on Arthur's return.*) Ah, and here comes my wine, thank goodness. Arthur, your timing is excellent, as always, I see.

Arthur Thank you, sir. Do you want me to open it?

Wilde I most certainly do.

But Bosie is not letting go.

Bosie What? What are you saying exactly? You are

saying George Wyndham cannot succeed?

Wilde The outcome is settled. It makes no difference what we do now. (*He is suddenly fluent, at ease.*) Oh yes, by all means, admit your friend in his pinstripes, let him bring us news from the oak-panelled corridors of whispered meetings with all his biscuity, high-minded friends. But, Bosie . . . do you believe such meetings can weigh on our fortunes? Even you must see it, it's simply too late.

Bosie Too late?

Wilde Yes. Of course. Ask Robbie. There is no point in further discussion, because further discussion is plainly foredoomed.

Bosie I don't understand. Why do you say that?

Wilde Do you still not grasp it? I see it clearly, my God! Plainly, so plainly! With the force of revelation.

Bosie Oscar, what makes you so sure that you're not going to win?

Wilde throws up his hands, near tears.

Wilde Oh . . .

Ross Look, Bosie . . .

Bosie No, really. There are two things we seem to be glibly assuming. First, that there *will* be a criminal trial. And, second, that, should it take place, we are destined to lose it.

Wilde Bosie, do you really imagine I care? Do you think it is the prospect of *losing* which makes me so fearful?

Bosie moves towards him with genuine compassion.

Bosie Oh, Oscar, I beg you . . . I beg you, do not give up.

Wilde Give up? Give up? Why should it matter? 'Shall I

give up?' 'Shall I carry on?' Either? Neither? Guilty! Not guilty! How can it make a blind bit of difference? The simple fact is: I am cast in a role. My story has already been written. How I choose to play it is a mere matter of taste. The performance of the actor will not determine the action.

Bosie And what is this action?

Wilde The action is: I am being expelled!

He is suddenly savage. Bosie turns away.

Bosie Oh really!

Wilde It's true. I am trapped in the narrative. The narrative now has a life of its own. It travels inexorably towards my disgrace. Towards my final expulsion. And it bears me along on its crest . . . (*He seems suddenly almost exhilarated.*) Yes, in fact, for me, borne along by this story, there is even an odd kind of freedom. I may wear whatever mask I may choose. Tragic? Defiant? Tearful? Resigned? I may try all these attitudes. I may bring what so-called 'feelings' I like to the role. But they will not have the slightest effect on the outcome. The story has only one possible end.

Bosie is genuinely frightened now.

Bosie Oscar, why do you feel that? For God's sake! After all we have been through! Just see him! What may you lose by it? My cousin is serious. My cousin is desperately concerned.

At this Wilde seems to relax, as if on familiar territory.

Wilde Of course. I do not for one second doubt it. I know that look in the English. They affect a particular furrow-browed earnestness, a desperate considerateness. As they settle one's fate, they arrange their features in a way which is always moral and grave. They speak about law and principle and how much it will hurt them to do the thing they must do. And at the end of the seriousness, the weightiness, the sorrow, the judicious weighing of things in the scales – have you really not noticed? – the decisions they make lead only one way. This is England. There is always a hanging! And this time it's decided: the noose has been fitted and the neck is my own!

Arthur hovers with the bottle.

Arthur Do I pour, sir?

Wilde Pour. (*He is so absorbed he has not even turned to Arthur.*) Have you never once stopped . . . have you never asked yourself . . . never once wondered why your Wyndhams exist? Why they exhibit all that desperate doggy concern? Wyndhams exist only to stand in front of the Asquiths. And the Asquiths are the ones who get their own way.

A knock, and the door opens again. It is Mr Moffatt with a second trolley.

Ask Mr Moffatt. Mr Moffatt's not English. The English have been my subject for years. Oh yes, in England the preacher says prayers on the scaffold. Then straight after he dines with the hangman.

He turns as Phoebe joins Moffatt at the door.

And how appropriate! It seems that the lobster is here.

Phoebe has a large tray with a silver dome. Arthur joins Mr Moffatt, who has a trolley with saucepans and a burner.

And it is the lovely Phoebe who brings it . . .

Phoebe Thank you, sir.

Wilde Robbie, please shower her with money at once. Alter my mood! Let us do something noble! Let us try and change Phoebe's life for the good.

Phoebe Sir.

Phoebe is blushing with pleasure. Bosie moves away in despair.

Wilde Since we ourselves cannot be happy . . .

Ross Oh, Oscar . . .

Wilde . . . let another be happy instead. Yes? You agree with me, Phoebe?

Phoebe I'd quite like some money, sir, if that's what you mean.

Moffatt, busying for elaborate meal preparation, looks disapprovingly.

Moffatt Phoebe . . .

Phoebe I'm sorry, sir. I didn't mean to say that. I hope I gave no offence.

Wilde You did not. You could not.

Phoebe Thank you, sir.

For a second, it seems he might reach out and touch her. They are both moved.

Wilde Robbie, open my pocketbook forthwith.

Ross No, I refuse to.

Wilde What, would you defy me?

Moffatt Sir, would you like us to serve you the lobster at once?

Wilde Lay it forth, by all means. Yes, now is the moment.

Moffatt I'll do it, sir.

Wilde Light up your fire and release some warmth in our hearts!

Moffatt lights the silver spirit lamp, which gives a big pop.)

There we are. The flame of Olympia! A little beacon of hope that flickers and flares . . .

Moffatt And shall I ready the sauce, sir?

Wilde Set to, Mr Moffatt. Abduct me down the path of excess!

Moffatt Yes, sir.

The three staff all laugh, busy round the trolley, as Moffatt prepares the sauce for the lobster. Wilde moves over to Bosie and speaks quietly.

Wilde Oh, Bosie, I beg you, do not look so sulky. I cannot bear to see you cast low.

Bosie Well, how do you want me to take this?

Wilde In the same way I hope I will take it myself.

An intimacy has returned. Wilde reaches out and touches his hand.

Bosie . . .

Bosie I cannot. Oscar, you know what I feel for you. You have been the luck of my life. But now you are taking up an attitude that makes no sense to me. You have decided you are foredoomed. It is as if you want your own downfall. You welcome it. (*He looks to Ross, suddenly an ally.*) Oscar imagines this weakness poetic, it is what he has called embracing his fate . . .

Wilde Is that right?

Bosie How you love that idea! But to me it has no such attraction. It just means that you lack the will to fight back.

> *Wilde is close to Bosie. Ross watches. The three staff go on with their work.*

In your writing you love to say there is always a destiny. Men are always dragged down by the gods. Do not make this mistake. Do not confuse your life with your art. Such ideas belong only in literature. They do not belong in the world. (*He leans further in, assured, not wanting the hotel servants to hear.*) These boys . . . these boys who will testify, who will stand up in court and say you took them to bed . . . who are they? They are known to be renters. Blackmailers. The scum of society. Why do you think that the court will believe them? Why are you so sure you cannot then win?

Wilde I have said. I am indifferent to winning. Whatever the verdict, my reputation is gone.

Bosie Ah yes, of course, how convenient. It's all a conspiracy! The disaster has happened already, and of course it's not your own fault. How easy! It's always the fault of the English. The English who are obsessed with claiming your scalp . . .

> *Wilde moves away in despair at this.*

Wilde Oh, Bosie, Bosie . . .

Bosie But I do well to remind you, if you go down, then I will go down by your side. You've forgotten. I am also a poet as well. But with a far different outlook. I don't find destruction romantic.

> *Wilde looks up at his accusation.*

Yes. It is true, and I mean it. Yesterday, in court, those answers you gave. You have wanted this thing. In some terrible part of you. You have welcomed the chance to play tragedy. (*He has moved closer again to Wilde.*) Well then, please sit in this room until you are groggy. By all means. Until you are musky with drink. Sit here and tell yourself that your fate is decided. The whole thing is written in advance in the stars! But I am a different character. I know you better than anyone alive. You always sit there, you always leave it to others to act. I'm sick of it. I'm sick of you. I shall confer with my cousin. Because, unlike you, Oscar, I want to fight.

Bosie goes out. Wilde is devastated by his departure.

Moffatt Sir, the meal is now ready.

Wilde Ah . . .

Moffatt The dish is prepared.

Wilde Good.

The table is set out like a vision, but Wilde does not move towards it.

Moffatt The lobster has been softened in butter. Tomatoes have been added, crushed garlic, shallots, tarragon, orange peel, parsley, white wine . . .

Wilde Yes, thank you.

Moffatt We dust with cayenne and then bathe in fresh cream.

Wilde Please. (*He still does not move.*) In one moment I will be ready to eat it. Robbie, I insist you reward them at once.

But Ross is ready to stand firm.

Now, Robbie . . . give me that pocketbook. Give me my cash, I insist. Give it here. You must hand it over. I have to remind you the money is mine.

Ross No, I won't.

Wilde Robbie . . .

Ross I cannot do it in honesty. The money is there to fund you in exile. I cannot allow you to give it away.

The three go very still, sensing the tension as Wilde moves towards Ross.

Wilde Robbie, just pass me the pocketbook. Earlier I asked you to cash me a cheque . . .

Ross I did it.

Wilde Well?

Ross That cheque was intended for one purpose only.

Wilde Its purpose is not your concern.

Ross Oscar, this is what Bosie is saying. You do not protect your own cause. You need this money. With all respect to these people, why would you waste it?

Wilde Give me my money! How dare you? The money is mine!

Wilde has shouted this, and is now swaying slightly. Moffatt is uncomfortable.

Moffatt Excuse me, sir . . .

Wilde No, Mr Moffatt, this does not concern you. Robbie, give me my money.

Ross No, I refuse.

Wilde moves closer. Ross is transfixed.

Wilde Robbie, come close to me. Robbie. Would you wish to upset me? Now, Robbie. Robbie. Look me in the eye. It is my will. Give me the pocketbook.

There is a silence. Ross reaches into his breast pocket and hands the wallet over.

Thank you. Please allow us all to live our own lives.

He moves a little unsteadily towards the group, who are standing together.

Mr Moffatt, I have had magnificent service. I have remarked on this already, I know. But the vision of this meal reminds me . . . the standard of service is the highest I've known. For that reason, I would be grateful . . . it would do me honour if I could bestow some reward . . . (*Fumblingly, he takes out notes.*) For the three of you, say, five pounds for your trouble? Ten, even? Five each?

Wilde has misread Moffatt's reluctance and clumsily taken out more.

Moffatt I'm sorry, Mr Wilde, but we cannot accept.

The group stirs. Wilde is shocked.

Wilde What?

Moffatt No, sir, we cannot. We cannot take this money of yours. If we accepted, it would weigh on our conscience. No, really. I promise, I speak for us all. Arthur?

Arthur Indeed, sir.

Moffatt Phoebe?

Phoebe Yes, I feel the same way.

It is not true for Phoebe, and they all know it.

Moffatt These last few weeks, Mr Wilde, we have come to know you. No visitor to this hotel has ever been kinder or better regarded than you. And not for what you have given us. Not money, anyway. You have given us kindness. And at this moment your need is greater than ours.

Here, in this hotel, we see all sorts of people. People of every background and type. But we see very few gentlemen.

He bows very slightly. Wilde, near to tears again, is barely able to speak.

Wilde Thank you. I am very moved.

Moffatt And now we would ask you just one single favour . . .

Wilde Of course. What's that, Mr Moffatt?

Moffatt That you sit down and eat your lunch.

Wilde Yes, of course, Mr Moffatt.

He sits down obediently. They hand him his napkin. They pour wine into his glass. A small ritual. Then:

Moffatt We'll leave you. Goodbye, sir. Call if there's anything you feel you might need.

All Three Goodbye, sir.

Moffatt We will be close, sir.

Wilde Thank you. Thank you indeed.

They go out. Wilde has lifted his fork but then he breaks down, overcome.

I cannot. I cannot eat it. (*He drops the fork and gets up, moving blindly towards Ross.*) Oh, Robbie, Robbie . . .

Ross Oscar . . .

Wilde Robbie, come here, please, come here and hold me . . .

Ross Oh, Oscar . . .

Wilde Hold me, my dear, my precious, my own . . .

45

The two men stand in each others' arms.

Ross Oh, Oscar . . .

Wilde You think . . . you think I have upset Bosie? What is Bosie thinking, do you know?

Ross I do not.

Wilde has buried his head in Ross's shoulder, but now Ross tenses and Wilde moves away, the moment passed.

Wilde Good God, what's happening? I am awash. I have lost my handkerchief. Oh Lord, are there handkerchieves here? (*He has blundered over to the suitcase and is now pulling at its contents, clothes going everywhere in his untidy search.*)

Ross Please, Oscar, let me. I packed a bunch of silk hand-kerchieves Constance gave me . . .

Wilde Oh, Constance, oh Lord . . .

Wilde moves away and lets Ross take over in the suit-case.

Even the sound of her name. Look! Even the lobster reproaches me. Everything reproaches me. Look, just look at its dead eye staring up. To have killed me, it says, and then not even to eat me!

Coldly, Ross hands him a handkerchief.

Ross Oscar, I'm afraid the moment has come.

Wilde It's come?

Ross has gone back to put everything into the bag and close it up.

Ross By my watch it's now just gone three-fifteen. Remember, you don't yet have a ticket. If we leave now you will still have a chance.

Wilde Yes. (*He is wiping his tears away as he moves across the room.*) Now?

Ross Yes.

Wilde You think? How can I leave without Bosie? I can hardly leave without saying goodbye.

Ross Soon enough you may see him.

Wilde I cannot leave if Bosie feels it is wrong.

Ross shifts, containing his temper.

Forgive me, I do not feel fully at ease. It is an instinct, no more. I look. I imagine myself as I pass through that door. (*He looks for a moment, then waves a hand.*) No. Not yet. I need to speak once more to Bosie. Yes. Bring me Bosie and then I will go.

He has sat down. Ross is holding the packed bag, ready to go.

Ross Oscar, I am uncertain why you are so keen to delay your departure . . .

Wilde I have given my reasons. I still am not sure.

Ross I can only say if you do not leave quickly – if you do not leave in the next five minutes, in fact – the chances are that tonight you will spend your first night in prison. This is a prospect I do not believe you have faced.

Wilde is silent a moment.

Wilde I have faced it.

Ross Oh really? (*He puts the bag down, intense, serious.*) I have been waiting, I have been standing here desperately trying not to say this all week. You are locked in a quarrel not of your making! You have done all you have to. Your duty is over and now you must leave!

Wilde sinks deeper into his chair, resentful.

Your friends, yes, your real friends have all tried to tell you . . .

Wilde I have not lacked for the telling!

Ross They have tried to warn you. You have walked open-eyed towards this disaster. (*He is nodding, not to be diverted.*) If you just stop, if you stop and consider, if you give a moment's thought to how Bosie has actually behaved . . . like sending his father a telegram. He called his own father 'a funny little man'!

Wilde looks away, impatient.

It's as if he has deliberately been stoking this quarrel. Do you think his father was not bound to react? You yourself told us he flaunted a revolver . . .

Wilde Oh . . .

Ross Yes. He took out a revolver, he waved it around in the Berkeley Hotel. Then he said – in the hearing of everyone – 'Please tell my father to come here and face me.'

Wilde I told him. It was stupid. (*Wilde looks at Ross resentfully.*)

Ross Bosie was issuing a challenge. He was piling up insults, he never missed a chance for public abuse. Do you think he didn't know what outcome was likely? His sole and single intention was always to make his father respond.

Wilde looks at him, unable to reply.

Yes, and when he had succeeded, when he had goaded his father to a point which he simply could not ignore, then it was not Bosie who was threatened. It was not Bosie who had to risk all in court. Oh no! Instead the boy turns to his dearest friend Oscar and says: 'Could you possibly do this on my behalf?'

Wilde That isn't true.

Ross Oh, isn't it? And that you, Oscar Wilde, so puissant, so brilliant, should be pulled along like a poodle! Where are you? Where is the Oscar we knew? (*He has hurt Wilde, but goes on regardless.*) And now you're delaying because he wants you to stay here! Of course! Stay here in England? Why not? It's your life, not his. You are to stay here and confront this famous list of immoral young men. Yet one thing we're forgetting: how did you meet them? I'm asking. How did you meet them?

Wilde looks sullen, not answering.

You choose not to answer because you know full well you cannot.

Wilde All right!

Ross You choose not to say it but you met them through *him*. Yes! And will *he* face prosecution?

Wilde Now, Robbie . . .

Ross Will *his* life be dragged through the courts? No, of course not. He escapes. When he has done these same things and with these same men. (*He is upset by his own cruelty.*) Why does Bosie escape prosecution?

Wilde Robbie . . .

Ross He escapes prosecution because he's a lord! Well, it's true and you know it! When I met you, you knew none of these young men. It was Bosie who drew you into this trade. And why? Because Bosie withheld himself.

Wilde Robbie, you must not go on with this. You have said quite enough!

Ross sits on the bed. There is a silence, then he speaks again more quietly.

Ross I have watched you. You are intent on denying reality. Now you ask of your friends that we should deny it as well. I heard you today, you yourself said it, nothing but trouble waits for you now. This is your moment. Save yourself, Oscar. Make for the continent!

Wilde You demand that I make a decision. Here is my decision. I refuse to go until Bosie returns.

Ross leaves the room. Wilde gets up and pours himself another glass of wine. He stands at the table, the meal cooling in front of him. Then Ross returns.

Ross He will not be long. (*He sits on the bed.*) Oscar, there are other people who love you. Perhaps you should remember there are others as well.

Wilde looks at him, then speaks quietly.

Wilde What is the fatal human passion? What is the source of all sin on this earth? This propensity in all human beings to indulge in the improper rapture, the gratuitous pleasure of giving others advice. Yes, I had rather swim neck-deep in London's arterial sewer, I had rather give up my body to every diseased and indigent tramp in the street, than surrender to this abominable indulgence of telling other people what they should do.

Ross looks down, rebuked.

It is not kind. It is not kind of you, Robbie. Is there not some small part of us which is purely our own? Which is our soul? Which is our innermost being? And which we alone should control? You bombard me. It is not fair. In any civilized war unfortified places are respected. I knew what you thought. You did not need to tell me. You know full well: I have done what I did out of love.

Ross looks back at him, saying nothing.

Do not . . . do not seek to destroy me by laying out what you call the facts. It is cruel of you, Robbie, it is cruel when you do such a thing. I have acted out of love. I have defended this love which exists between us, the purest I have known in my life. More perfect, more vital, more telling, more various, richer, more vibrant, more sweet. The redeeming fact of my life. (*He turns and looks at Ross.*) It is what I have left. It is what remains to me. All else has now been taken away. So you would now take even that from me. You would tell me I have been deceived and used in all this? Consider what you are saying. If the love between us is not as I think it, then I shall have suffered to no purpose at all.

Bosie appears. His manner has changed completely. The certainty has been replaced by a considerate gentleness.

Bosie Oscar . . .

Wilde Ah, Bosie . . .

Bosie I'm sorry. I have kept you too long.

Wilde Not at all.

Bosie I have been talking to George in the corridor.

Wilde Well?

Bosie I'm afraid his news is not helpful. He has failed. He says that you will be arrested.

There is a slight pause as Bosie waits for Wilde to take this in.

He says, however, there is one further thing you should know.

Wilde What is that?

Bosie They are deliberately choosing to delay.

Wilde They're delaying?

Bosie Yes. Till this evening. George says they are employing a sporting metaphor. The fox must be given its chance to escape.

Wilde is taken aback, but he sounds distant when he replies.

Wilde Oh, I see.

Bosie They would prefer it. It would suit them better if you would flee. This brief opening is offered.

Wilde How considerate! And, Bosie, tell me, what do you think I should do?

Bosie shifts, not really liking this direct question.

No, really. I'm asking. No, truly.

Bosie But surely you must decide.

Wilde Surely. But you must still have an opinion. Well?

Bosie is still not at ease.

Bosie You know I would prefer you to stay here. Nothing George tells me has changed how I think. I still am persuaded that if we pursue it with vigour, there is no question the case can be won.

Wilde Yes.

Bosie But the point is that just at this moment . . . just at this moment itself . . . George is saying that when they come to arrest you, it is in nobody's interest that I myself should be here.

Wilde nods judiciously.

Wilde No.

Bosie If it is known . . . if it is known in the newspapers that you and I were together at the time of arrest . . .

Wilde Yes, of course . . .

Bosie Then that is something which George says will surely further inflame my father and therefore make this whole matter worse.

Wilde I see. (*He looks at Bosie, thoughtful.*)

Bosie Now look . . . I have said . . . if you want me to stay with you, there is no question I will. I belong at your side. But in what he's suggesting I confess I do see a sort of brutal wisdom.

Wilde Yes. I discern that brutal wisdom myself.

Bosie takes a step towards him.

Bosie Be clear. I'm not for one second abandoning you.

Wilde No.

Bosie I hope you know me.

Wilde I know you, of course.

Bosie I am leaving for only this interval. I say again. This brief interval, no more and no less. (*He looks down before giving more news.*) George wants me to go with him to Westminster. He wants me to work with him on your behalf. He thinks he may secure you bail for tonight. Assuming of course that you do not flee.

Wilde looks at him, almost as if not understanding.

Wilde We could meet tonight?

Bosie Yes.

Wilde We could meet this evening?

Bosie If you stay, nothing changes. We meet as we always have done. You may be assured. It is the wish of my heart. (*Bosie hesitates before more bad news.*) George is saying . . . he is saying my family would like me to travel. They would prefer it if I too went away. But I have told him: no, if Oscar stays, then I shall stay with him. (*He has moved closer to Wilde and now looks straight at him.*) I shall not leave you.

Wilde No. (*He is strangely absent, as if looking at Bosie properly for the first time.*)

Bosie Have you decided?

Wilde I'm sorry?

Bosie Today. Will you stay or go?

Wilde Oh. I am in the process, Bosie. Kiss me.

Bosie moves across to him and kisses him. The kiss deepens. Then Wilde withdraws a little and hugs him. There is silence.

It is what we fear which happens to us.

Arthur knocks, then opens the door.

Arthur Sir, excuse me, it's Mr Wyndham. He says Lord Alfred must join him now. He says it's urgent. He cannot wait any longer.

Wilde Yes, thank you, Arthur.

Arthur He asked me to insist Lord Alfred must leave here at once. (*He stands, waiting.*)

Bosie I'm sorry . . .

Wilde I know. You have no time now. Bosie . . .

Bosie Yes. I must leave.

Wilde spreads his arms in a sudden access of cheerfulness.

Wilde So. We shall meet again but we cannot say when. However. My darling, may it be soon.

Bosie I must go. I must go. (*He smiles helplessly, boyish now, laughing at the absurdity of it.*) Oh God, what a business! No, truly. Yes, may it be soon. I'm sorry. I'm sorry. As the French say, *à bientôt*.

He goes out, all breathless charm, and Arthur closes the door.

Wilde So. They choose to offer me this opening. The whole world wants me to go.

Ross Yes.

Wilde The world persists in thinking me shallow. They think me feckless. They consider me weak. Flee, and I hand them this ready opinion. Do you know I think I may have decided? (*He moves to the wine, resolved.*) Open my case, I beg you. I wish to sit here. I wish to read. I shall not run down this hole they have dug for me. I will not stoop to leave on all fours.

Ross puts the cases back on the bed in despair.

Yes. I can run but I choose not to. Die of embarrassment in some hovel abroad? Admit to society they have driven me out? No, I will not give them that pleasure. I am going to do the single thing which will drive them to frenzied distraction: I am going to sit down and get on with my lunch. (*He sits rather clumsily down at the table and contemplates the meal in front of him.*) My mind is made up. Good. A book. Yes, a book, please, Robbie.

Ross re-opens the case to get him a book. Wilde lifts his knife and fork, but for a moment they are suspended.

If I run now, my story is finished. For as long as I stay it is not at an end. I prefer my story unfinished. (*He turns and looks at Ross*.) Robbie, we shall not discuss it. I shall eat and the train will make its own way. Do you hear? Do you hear that whistle? (*He lifts a hand to his ear and waits*.) Do you hear the wheels running away down the track? What is that? The train is departing. Do you sense the life we did not live? (*He starts to tuck happily into the lobster*.) This lobster's good.

Ross It was better earlier.

Wilde I'm sure. I could not eat it before.

Ross moves across the room in agony.

Robbie, you know you must leave me also. It is not safe for you here.

Ross I know that.

Wilde You have done enough. You must not be found with me.

Ross No. I promised my mother . . .

Wilde You as well . . .

Ross Yes. This morning I promised. If you were arrested, I promised I would not be there. She said if I am with you when you are arrested I will be ruined for ever.

Wilde goes on eating contentedly.

Wilde I'm sure your mother knows about these things.

Ross Well, I have always done what my mother said. (*He has said this with a smile. Now he takes off his topcoat*.) But if Bosie cannot be with you. If it seems that Bosie cannot stay . . .

Wilde glances briefly from his eating. Ross sits down in an armchair.

. . . then I am not willing to leave you.

Wilde Good. I shall not be alone. (*He puts down his knife and fork.*) The food is good. The book is excellent. We know the police have been delayed. Once more it seems I have no alternative. I have no other option. It is clear. The moment has come when I must sleep.

Ross You cannot sleep!

Wilde Why not?

Ross They will come to arrest you.

Wilde I am tired. (*He has got up from the table and lain down on the sofa, with only his wine beside him.*)

Ross They will find you like this.

Wilde It suits me. I do not care for their judgement at all. (*He closes his eyes. The room grows dark. Music has started to play quietly again.*) Let us sleep and dream of trains now . . .

Ross I'll sit.

Wilde Let us sleep. Let us sleep and dream of tunnels, too. Let us hear that metal clacking along the track.

> *He is about to fall asleep on the sofa. Ross sits, keeping guard over him.*

For as long as we sleep we are in safety. The train is going. And I shall sleep.

> *The music begins to fill out. The room is darkened, but light comes again from the high window and sweeps round in a circle, like the transit of the sun catching the dust in the air, or the deep yellow beam of a lighthouse, highlighting the room exquisitely, as it passes and dies.*
>
> *Then, after a while, light returns to the room itself. They have not yet lit the lamps, so they are silhouetted by the light of a cold London afternoon from the window.*

Ross does not realize that Wilde has opened his eyes.
SCENE TWO.

You are still here.

Ross Yes.

Wilde Do you remember? Do you remember when we first met?

Ross Yes.

Wilde You seduced me.

Ross Yes.

Wilde You were the first man I slept with. Yet I imagined I knew more than you.

There is a knock and Arthur is again at the door.

Arthur Sir . . .

Ross Yes?

Arthur There's a reporter. He says the police are just about to arrive. They are coming upstairs to take you. He says they are on their way.

Wilde Thank you, Arthur. Will you light the lamps for us?

Arthur goes round and lights the lamps in the room. Wilde has sat up on the sofa and now he gets up. Ross does not move.

I am well ready. Robbie?

Ross Yes.

Wilde You are at my side.

Arthur goes on lighting lamps.

Arthur, when the police arrive, then please admit them.

Arthur Yes, sir.

Wilde takes the book Ross gave him earlier.

Wilde Ready?

Ross Yes.

Arthur stands at the door waiting. Wilde sits down, and starts reading the book. It is an image of the solidest Victorian contentment. Wilde turns a page, calm.

Wilde Let them come in.

Act Two: Deciding to Leave

SCENE ONE. *Friday 3 December 1897. The music is serene as Italian light floods into the Villa Guidice at Posillipo, near Naples. It is late afternoon. The sun is an astonishing wintry gold outside the double doors which lead on to the balcony. The style is seaside vernacular. You can see a white metal rail. There is a sense of sun, sea and the horizon. Inside, modernism. The walls are white. The sparse furniture of the rented house looks forward, in its coolness and pallor, to the twentieth century. The main door gives on to a small hallway, with stairs beyond. The room is uncluttered, with one small table on which there is a pot of coffee, some cups and some sugared buns.*

Wilde is sitting in a chair reading. He is dressed like an English gentleman in very formal, dark clothes, which make no concessions to the Mediterranean. His body has grown slack and fat and his face is ravaged by deprivation and alcohol. There is a tension in his movements which is new. Behind him, on a pale sofa, two men are sleeping under a sheet. They have plainly been there some time. There are clothes on the floor. One of them stirs and we see that it is Bosie. He is now past his mid-20s and still good-looking, but no longer radiant with youth. Bosie sits up, taking a moment to wake, but Wilde just carries on reading.

Bosie We never made it upstairs.

Wilde It does not bother me at what level you do it. Please perform at any elevation you choose. To me it's a matter of consummate indifference.

Bosie has sat up. The Young Man stirs beside him. A mop of thick, curly dark hair, and a body plainly young and fit.

He looks like the young fisherman.

Bosie He is. That's who he is. That's what he does.

Wilde Can you ask him: is there any chance of a red mullet? (*He lights a cigarette.*) It would be nice for the whole household to profit from the encounter.

Bosie He doesn't fish red mullet.

Wilde Ah. Choosy, is he? A herring, then?

The Young Man has woken, and gets out of bed. Naked, but not fazed, he sees Wilde.

Good afternoon. I am the great Irish poet and dramatist, Oscar Wilde.

Young Man *Mi scusi. Sono venuto a casa sua senza invito.*

Wilde *Non fa niente. Lei è il benvenuto a casa mia.*

They have shaken hands. The Young Man goes unselfconsciously out on to the balcony to stretch.

Ah, all the modesty of an Italian, I see. A generative organ like a rope that has been dipped in pitch and, to judge from the look on your face, also the deep, instinctive understanding of the needs of English aristocracy necessary to go with it.

Bosie How you love that word.

Wilde Which word?

Bosie Aristocracy. (*He has wrapped the sheet round himself and gone over to the little table.*) What time is it?

Wilde Five o'clock. Yes. In the afternoon. (*He throws Bosie a quick glance.*) It's been another achingly beautiful day. Light dancing on the surface of the sea. A watery sun and only the slightest cool in the evening to tell you that winter is here. The Bay of Naples jewelled like the scrawny neck of some ageing dowager.

The Young Man has come back into the room and is helping himself to a sugared bun.

All the native dignity of his race, and then that fabulous cock as well . . .

Bosie gets up and goes out.

Bosie The coffee's cold.

Wilde Yes, well it was hot at ten o'clock this morning. (*He calls to Bosie in the kitchen.*) What's his name?

Bosie (*off*) Galileo.

Wilde Ah. See stars, did you?

Bosie returns at once and sits, still in a dream. Galileo has gone to sit naked on the floor, with legs crossed, his back against the end of the sofa, looking out the window. He eats his bun happily.

Oh, it's wonderful, it's like a child, isn't it? Who said one can never go back? If only I could go back to that! If I ever was like that! Like an animal, like a cat. Truly, one should throw him a ball of string. Look at the little fellow.

Bosie You know nothing.

Wilde Sometimes one is hard put to believe in the idea of human progress. Just three hundred years ago the name Galileo was attached to an intelligence that powered the Renaissance and took mankind to an understanding of his own condition to which he had never previously dared to aspire. The heavens opened for Galileo. Today show us a Galileo and we see a kitten on the floor.

Galileo has turned at the repeated mention of his name.

Yes, Galileo, we are talking about you.

Galileo *Che state dicendo?*

Wilde *Sei fortunato di poter' vivere vicino al mare, e poter' camminare ogni giorno sulla spiaggia.*

Galileo *Ah, si, si.*

Bosie is eating a bun at the table.

Bosie He's a wonderful man. I met his mother last night. And all his sisters. They live right by the beach. I went drinking with his fellow fishermen.

Wilde Will you meet all of them?

Bosie Eventually.

Wilde I can't wait.

Bosie is undisturbed by Wilde's gentle mockery. It is happy between them.

We can expect a succession of sofa-bound Renaissance geniuses, can we? All waking here tousle-haired and humanist in the afternoons.

Bosie Perhaps.

Wilde One day we play host to a Leonardo, next day a Michelangelo. Will there be a whole gallery of them? A sort of horizontal Uffizi. At the weekend perhaps we are at home to both Piero della Francesca *and* Gugliemo della Porto, maybe – who knows? – even both at once, but all distinguished from their eminent namesakes by the fact they have their bums in the air, and they're offered a sugar bun for their favours.

Bosie Why so superior? You like them as much as I do.

Wilde I do. All I cared for was beauty. I can still see it. From across a gulf. But I see it. (*He goodnaturedly stubs out his cigarette.*) You and I have no friends. Let us have lovers instead.

Galileo *Che cosa dici?*

Wilde Throw him another bun.

Bosie chucks him another.

C'è troppo zucchero?

Galileo *No, o' zuccher, me piac' assai. Poi, questi sono quelli buoni, freschi, ancora caldi. Li hai comprati da Gigi, li sull'angolo.*

Bosie What is he saying?

Wilde Why? Does it bother you?

Bosie No.

Wilde You seem to speak to him in his language, one way or another, even if that language in your case is not specifically Italian. My love.

They look at each other a moment.

Bosie What have you been doing?

Wilde Reading. My publisher has been kind enough to send me a list of proposed names for the foundation of a British Academy of Letters.

Bosie How ridiculous!

Wilde He keeps me in touch. (*He lifts a letter from beside him.*) He has enclosed what they call their proposed list of immortals. It is amusing stuff. Personally I cannot make my mind up between the claims of the Duke of Argyll and

Jerome K. Jerome. I think probably the former. The unread is always better than the unreadable.

Bosie Are they canvassing your vote?

Wilde Hardly, my dear.

Bosie glances quickly at Wilde who is lighting another cigarette.

Bosie And writing? Have you done some writing?

Wilde Of course. My play.

Bosie How is your play?

Wilde My play is first-class. (*He holds up another envelope.*) There is a letter for you.

Bosie From whom?

Wilde I'd say from your mother.

Bosie I will look at it later. Thank you.

Wilde puts it down.

Wilde Now, as for tonight . . .

Bosie Oh, please, we have seen every performance Duse has given.

Wilde We cannot playgo because we have no money.

Bosie None?

Wilde We have not a penny. I have been twice to the Post Office while you were practising astronomy . . .

Bosie And?

Wilde Nothing. Nothing has arrived.

Bosie (*frowns*) I thought you were expecting payment for your poem.

Wilde Indeed I am. I am pursuing it. I have written many times. My knee-pads are scuffed and scoured by the time I have spent in the supplicant's position. I eat the dirt off the floor. When I visit the Post Office there is a collective Italian groan . . . (*He raises his hands above his head.*) '*Ah, Signor Wilde, lo scrittore irlandese*, has returned once more, begging, screaming, squealing for money.' As I leave, ragamuffin children dance in the streets. The whole of Naples reverberates with their cries: 'There goes Signor Wilde, the famous Irish playwright, who has no money. No money! No money!'

Bosie looks seriously worried at this.

Bosie What do we have? What is left to us?

Wilde A few bottles of brandy. Some coffee. The last servant I have sent away. Beyond that, nothing. Unless there is a chance of your getting a ride on his boat tonight. Perhaps if you went fishing we would at least eat tomorrow. If you became a fisherman.

Bosie No one in my family has ever taken up the professions.

Wilde We can't live on cock.

Bosie nods at the letter again.

Bosie The letter from Mother. How thick is it?

Wilde There's no cheque in it. I have held it up to the light.

Bosie Well, then.

Galileo has finished his second bun.

Galileo *Che facite po riest d'o giorno?*

Wilde *Non abbiamo deciso. Vogliamo andare a teatro.*

Galileo *Teatro? Io, a teatro non ci posso andare. Ho tanto da fare, sono occupatissimo. Devo dare una mano a mio zio, giú al porto. Poi ho anche la sorella in ospedale. A teatro? Io? Come posso andare a teatro?*

Bosie looks to Wilde for a translation.

He is asking if I will go for a walk so that he can bugger you again.

Bosie And what is your answer?

There is a silence. For the first time the air is cool between them.

Wilde No.

Bosie looks at him. Then goes out to the kitchen. Wilde stubs out his cigarette.

Beauty? Yes. Beauty above everything, and in all things. So much I was right about, you see. Before the catastrophe, before the great disaster, one writes but one does not know. Until one has suffered, until the great suffering, it is all guesswork. One guesses merely. Imagination: a highfalutin word for guesswork.

He smiles. Galileo is content, half-listening, not understanding a word.

And, by and large, my guesses were right. There is no morality in what is called morality; there is no sense in what is called sense; and least of all is there meaning in what is held to be meaning. I saw this. Before I even suffered. And, suffering, found it to be true. I began an essay on the pleasures of alcohol. The purpose of alcohol being, as I understand it, to create full-blown beauty where, sober, it is only hinted at. The foolishness of people who say mere beauty. Like mere wit. Or mere being alive. (*He nods towards the kitchen.*) The man next door, making

67

the coffee, being, as both of us know, exquisitely beautiful and seeming therefore to hold some secret which must be prised from him. But which cannot, I fear, dear friend, be prised in a single night. (*He pauses.*) Nor even in a single life.

Bosie returns with a full pot of coffee.

Bosie Hot coffee.

Wilde Enjoy it. We are not yet boiling acorns, but in a few days . . .

Bosie You don't seem very worried.

Wilde What do you mean?

Bosie By not having any money.

Wilde Ah. I came at your invitation. If you remember, it was your idea. You promised to look after me. You had money, you said.

Bosie So? Who found the house?

Wilde You did.

Bosie Who paid? At least, who intended to pay? It is not my fault.

Wilde No. The roulette wheel disobliged again.

Bosie Well? We *could* have been rich.

Wilde Ah yes.

Bosie I could have doubled my money!

Wilde If only your success at gambling could equal your grasp of gambling's governing principles.

Bosie has gone back to pour himself hot, thick coffee.

'It can double my money!' Very good! You have understood the potential of the activity perfectly. You understand its lure. You know what it promises. And yet for some reason . . .

Bosie Very funny . . .

Wilde . . . you seem not to be able to make that little leap . . .

Bosie All right . . .

Wilde . . . that some people make: the leap to where it delivers what it promises. Why is that? What is that in you? The promise, but not the fulfilment of the promise . . .

Bosie looks at him defensively.

Bosie What are you saying?

Wilde I am saying you promised to look after me, Bosie. Yet the tradesmen's bills arrive with my name on the envelope. In restaurants, in bars, waiters turn to me. My pockets empty, not yours.

Bosie If I had money, I would give it to you. You know that. I have given you everything. Do you doubt my good faith?

Wilde No. Never.

After a moment, Bosie is quiet, serious.

Bosie Everyone left you, remember?

Wilde I do.

Bosie The virtuous Constance . . .

Wilde Ah yes . . .

Bosie . . . of whom we all heard so much. The embodiment of virtue, so-called. Faithful, long-suffering Constance . . . where was she? Robbie Ross, the good

69

friend, little Robbie. The trusted adviser, who loved you, who would give up his life for you . . . where was he? Abroad. All your so-called friends, so-called allies . . . Abroad! Scattered across Europe! Remember?

Wilde smiles slightly.

Wilde You left also.

Bosie Yes. But I was the last to go. Bear that in mind. I was the last.

Wilde I know.

Galileo looks up, catching the seriousness.

Galileo *Ma che sta dicendo?*

Wilde *È arrabbiato.*

Bosie is at the table, cradling the hot cup in his hands.

Bosie And yet only *I* am mocked. Everywhere! Your worthless friend! 'Feckless Bosie.' 'Shallow Bosie.' Oh yes, it is always I who am traduced. But it is I who stayed, who stayed by you until the day of your trial. (*He looks at Wilde.*) Yes. At least you were tried.

Wilde I was.

Bosie You were fortunate. I have been condemned, and yet I have not even been tried.

Wilde No. (*He is quiet, letting Bosie's mood pass.*)

Bosie I am much misrepresented.

Wilde I know that.

Bosie Even now, in the papers, all across Europe . . . how can I be what they say I am?

Wilde You are not.

Bosie They disregard my poetry. They disregard my status.

Wilde Indeed.

Bosie Your poetical equal, you said. You have said it in print. Your *equal*.

Wilde Just so.

   Bosie waits, wanting more.

It is true. I have said it. You are one of the greatest poets in England.

Bosie One of? *One* of?

Wilde Well, let us allow that Swinburne is living. Let us allow that Swinburne is alive.

Bosie *Swinburne?*

Wilde I know. But there is a school of thought, plainly backward, plainly misguided, which hands him the palm.

Bosie But you are not of it?

Wilde No. I am of your party.

Bosie Good. And so you should be. I am already the greatest non-narrative poet in England.

Wilde Undoubtedly. Your lyrics are lovely.

   Bosie is satisfied and goes on.

Bosie And let it be said, let it be made clear: I am as much the victim of this affair as you. Yes! Quite as much.

Wilde (*quietly*) In your own way.

Bosie Yes – oh yes – everywhere it is said: 'The incomparable tragedy of Oscar Wilde!' How easily said! And how lazily! Because, remember, two have suffered here . . .

Wilde Plainly.

Bosie And in many ways – I am not ashamed to say this – my suffering has been the greater. Oh yes, I know how that sounds, for I have not suffered physically . . .

Wilde No.

Bosie I know that. I would not say that.

Wilde Quite.

Bosie I have not known the deprivations of confinement . . .

Wilde You have not.

Bosie The squalor of the filthy prison cell. Not at all. But you, Oscar, have not known the horror of not being heard, of being disregarded, of being overlooked. The contempt of my peers! My God, is that not equal suffering? There are two people here!

Wilde I know that.

Bosie Two people who suffer and endure! Two human beings! (*His anger is rising dangerously.*) But that is not said in the papers.

Wilde No.

Bosie They speak only of the one who stood in the dock. God, how I long to set this whole affair right! God, I long to speak!

Wilde You must not speak. When you have spoken it has been a mistake. When you have published . . . (*He pauses, uneasy at the memory.*) When you have tried to publish certain private things between us . . . references to us, to our friendship, it has not advanced our cause.

Bosie Not advanced it?

Wilde No.

Bosie How is our cause advanced by our forbearance?

72

How is it helped? Is it helpful, do you think, never to say anything . . . never to speak of our lives?

Wilde shrugs slightly in reply.

How will things be changed . . . how will England be changed unless we speak?

Wilde Changing England is low on my list of current priorities.

Bosie What, are we to spend our whole lives shrouded in secrecy, covering our offence in shame?

Wilde So it appears.

Bosie Never daring to speak, never daring to say: 'Yes, we are two men who believe in the highest form of love – the purest, the most poetical, such as that which exists between us'? Love between men? Can we not speak of that?

Wilde Certainly not. Under no circumstances.

Bosie Why are you so sure?

Wilde Trust me. Truly. I understand this better than you. Trust me.

Galileo *Non capisco niente. Di che parlate?*

Wilde Nothing. *Niente.*

Galileo frowns, confused.

No. We have come to Naples to suffer and be silent. Ours is an ethic of silence. Preferably on a substantial private income. Which is, I admit, at this moment proving the elusive part of the plan.

Bosie Indeed.

Wilde However.

Bosie looks at him moodily.

Bosie You have no courage.

Wilde And you have no strategy. That is why we are perfectly suited. Let this conversation be over.

Bosie You always divert. You always turn away.

Wilde Why not?

Wilde has seen Bosie's bad mood off and now gestures towards the window. The light has begun to change.

The day has started to fade and turn dusky. The sun has begun its nightly cabaret . . .

Galileo *Vado a vestirmi. Nun pozz' sta ca' senza fa' nient.*

Wilde *Sei benvenuto a utilizzare il bagno.*

Galileo is gathering his clothes.

Let us attend to it. If we can no longer afford the great Duse, we must let nature provide the entertainment.

Bosie reaches out a hand to Galileo, which he squeezes before he goes out.

Last evening, the sun passed briefly through ochre, then, in a rare display of good taste, disdained primrose, and settled instead on a colour – oh Lord, I searched fifteen minutes on the balcony until I found the word. The sun was not like topaz. No. Nor was it the colour of saffron. I can only say to you with all the fleeting authority which my literary powers may still command that the sun was like orpiment. Have you heard that word?

Bosie Never.

Wilde is smiling, satisfied. And Bosie is watching fondly, drinking his coffee again.

74

Wilde So tonight, come, let us not spend the evening indoors in what my fellow Irishmen call begrudgery. Let us go out, let us walk among the youths again and enjoy the gorgeous vulgarity of the night. Yes?

Bosie As you wish.

Wilde It is nearing the hour when I cried every night in prison. I wept every night for a year. For the whole of my first year. At six o'clock.

Bosie watches him, serious now.

This is the hour Christ died.

Bosie I thought Christ died at three.

Wilde Christ died at six. He died at cocktail hour.

Suddenly there is the sound of a bell ringing at the door outside.

Bosie Ah, cocktails!

Wilde Oh Lord, are we expecting visitors?

Bosie No.

Wilde Surely not more fisherfolk? Are they coming to mend their nets in our living room? Will they gut sprats all over our floor?

He shudders in mock horror. Bosie has moved to collect up all his clothes.

Bosie We have no visitors, as well you know. Unless it's that woman who comes to deal with the rats.

Wilde More urgently, we have no servants. The social crisis is profound. A lord cannot answer the door. Will our friend answer for us, do you think? Can we ask him? Does he serve by land as well as by sea?

Bosie He serves.

The bell rings again. Bosie has gathered his things up. Wilde calls out.

Wilde *Galileo, per favore, puoi vedere chi c'è alla porta?*

Galileo (*off*) *Certo.*

Bosie smiles as he goes out of the room, passing Galileo on the stairs.

Bosie I suppose there is no question of *your* answering the door.

Wilde As you know, I have always disdained unnecessary motion.

Galileo opens the door and the visitor takes a step inside. It is Ross. He is paler and thinner than ever, in a light suit and hat. Wilde is taken aback.

(*quietly*) It's little Robbie.

Neither man moves. Bosie calls from upstairs.

Bosie (*off*) Who is it?

Wilde (*calls*) Robbie.

There is a second, then Bosie appears on the stairs. He has pulled on trousers and shirt. He is too angry to speak. After a few moments he goes back upstairs.

We did not know you were coming to Naples.

Ross Nor did I. (*He looks upstairs, disturbed by Bosie's silent disappearance.*) Oscar . . .

Wilde I am temporarily taken aback. We thought you were the witch.

Ross I'm sorry?

76

Wilde A witch comes to smoke out the rats. We are not much visited.

Ross I see.

Wilde This is a friend of Bosie's. His name is Galileo.

Galileo goes upstairs, saying nothing.

You did not favour us with a telegram.

Ross No. I was not sure you would see me.

Wilde Come, I will always see you. (*He gives Ross an icy smile. The light is becoming paler outside.*) We have not eaten for days, except stale sugar buns. But we have three bottles of brandy at least, and they are yours to enjoy.

Ross Thank you. Yes. I would like a glass.

Wilde Help yourself.

Ross moves nervously towards the brandy bottle on the side-table.

Bosie was remarking on my reluctance to move. He's right. My whole celebrity, you might say, is now based on that reluctance. I mean, not fleeing when you begged me to. Sitting still. Staying still. (*He lights another cigarette and settles deeper into the chair.*)

Ross You look well.

Wilde Do not mock me. My appearance is that of a senior pederastic Anglican bishop who has been locked all night in a distillery. Flatter me by all means, I adore it, but not for my appearance.

Ross busies himself at the table.

Do you bring us news of the arts? Does anyone still paint?

Ross Not in the way you would wish.

Wilde I am sure. The dissemination of photography which ought to release the artist from the drudgery of representation instead panics him into a dreary kind of rivalry.

Ross hands him some brandy in a glass like a tooth mug.

Thank you. We are living in dismal times.

Ross Hard times to make a living.

Wilde Please!

Ross For I am scarcely solvent myself.

Wilde You will prosper, Robbie. I predict. You have chosen exactly the right trade for the turn of the century. Art dealing holds snobbery, ignorance and greed in a near-miraculous equilibrium. Capitalism is the coming thing. I have seen enough to know.

Ross You mean, since your punishment?

Wilde Prison was not my punishment. This is my punishment. To your health.

Ross To yours.

They drink.

Wilde Where have you come from?

Ross Today? From Rome. Yesterday, from Nervi.

Wilde Ah yes. Now I understand. (*He looks at Ross, now knowing why he is here. The atmosphere toughens.*) You see how we are. You see how we are living.

Ross Yes.

Wilde Simply. The loan of a little money would help me.

Duse hopes to stage my play *Salome* but she needs investors.

Ross Again? You asked me before.

Wilde I did?

Ross Some months ago.

Wilde Plainly, my imagination is failing. (*He smiles, trying to recover.*) Was it Montaigne who said that the first qualification for a liar is that he must have a very good memory?

Ross Yes. It was Montaigne.

Wilde A loan is wasted either way, yet for some reason it reassures the giver to believe it is to be used what they call 'constructively'. Nobody lends five pounds for drugs, whereas everyone lends five pounds for an expedition to take young boys up the Zambezi.

Ross Not to you, Oscar. Not to you.

Wilde No. Nor to you, Robbie, when you were less of a prig.

Ross looks down at this overt hostility.

Never mind, I scramble on somehow, and hope to survive the winter. After that, Tunis, rags and hashish!

Ross It is not my fault. Truly.

But Wilde is not impressed by Ross's demeanour and remains aggressive.

Wilde Does it please you, this running between us?

Ross No.

Wilde Why do you do it, then?

Ross, pained, does not answer.

The behaviour of all my friends has begun to mystify me.

Ross When you came out of prison, everyone wanted to welcome you. They wanted to see you. We greeted you. We waited with flowers. We found you a house in France to live in!

Wilde So you are saying your friendship came with conditions?

Ross All friendship comes with conditions.

Wilde is dark, dismissive.

Wilde No. Myself, I gave friendship freely. To anyone. When I had it, I gave money away in the streets.

Ross Oscar, it is you who have made it hard for us.

Wilde So you say. (*He looks at Ross for a moment.*) Did you know my friend Dowson came out and took me to a brothel in Dieppe?

Ross No!

Wilde Yes. It was the first woman I had slept with in ten years. It was like chewing cold mutton. I said afterwards: 'The job is done. Tell of it in England for it will entirely restore my character.'

Ross smiles, but Wilde is unamused.

That is not my idea of friendship, Robbie.

Ross Oscar, I have tried to help you. I have tried at all times only to help you. My motives are pure. I seek only to reconcile parties who find it hard to be reconciled.

Wilde looks at him, still unimpressed.

Wilde I sense already you are bringing me bad news.

Ross I am bringing you news.

Wilde Ah . . .

Ross News I did not wish you to receive by letter. Whether it is bad or not depends on how you react to it.

Wilde Thank you. So it is my choice?

Ross Yes.

Wilde nods as if this confirmed his suspicions.

Wilde I have had indications. I have had letters. I have had threats. My trips to the Post Office reward me not with cheques but with cheap mottoes. My whole correspondence should be sponsored by the Salvation Army. It is relentlessly elevating.

Ross I have spoken to Constance.

Wilde Yes. Well, I imagined. How is she?

Ross Not well.

Wilde I heard.

Ross Her back is worse.

Wilde I am sorry.

Ross Her spine will not mend. It is broken from the fall. She is confined the whole day and the prognosis is that things will not improve.

Wilde takes this in for a moment.

Wilde And the children?

Ross Yes, she says the children are well.

Wilde Good.

Ross A little bewildered. Cyril is still in Heidelberg, Vyvyan in Monaco. They've learnt to play chess.

Wilde They ask after me?

Ross Often.

Wilde It is the hope of one day seeing them which sustains me. That is what sustains me. It is for that I live.

Ross Then we have common ground on which we can build.

Wilde looks at him suspiciously.

Constance says she has written.

Wilde She has. Often.

Ross She says you do not answer.

Wilde I have not answered, no.

Ross Why not?

Wilde I have nothing to say!

Ross You do not answer her letters!

Wilde What am I to say? That Duse is fine, but not as fine as Bernhardt? Art-chat? Art-gossip? The vagaries of the weather in Naples . . .

Ross She said she feared the worst when she heard you were in Naples. She said nobody goes to Naples at this time of year.

This remark inflames Wilde.

Wilde Plainly, Robbie, you have come to enrage me. You have come to unsettle me.

Ross No.

Wilde You have come to take her part.

Ross Why should I?

Wilde It is not enough to trap me – no, nor to try me – no, nor to send me to prison, to take away my reputation, my position, to take away my London, the London at whose very centre I once stood? This is now not enough. The world, having broken me, now must also come into my house? It will pursue me? It will not let up?

He stares at Ross fiercely, but Ross gives no ground.

Ross The means of it letting up are in your own hands.

Wilde In your view.

Ross No. In Constance's view.

Wilde And these views are not coincident? They are not the same?

Wilde has raised his voice, pressing Ross, but Ross is already shaking his head.

Ross Oscar, you know what you must do. You know what is asked of you.

Wilde Oh yes!

Ross I do not need to speak it. You know already. (*He moves across the room, containing his anger, and pours a second brandy.*)

Wilde What is this sense that I have let you all down in some way?

Ross I have not said that.

Wilde I would like to understand this. Explain to me. No, truly. You feel that somehow I have *failed* you? Is my offence that I am free? What would you wish? You would prefer me back in prison? (*He laughs at the absurdity of it.*) I am not just to live, but I must also live in a way of which you approve?

Ross Not I. Constance. I speak *to* Constance. I do not speak *for* her.

Wilde No? You mean you do not sit with her in Nervi, consoling her? You do not sit together in darkened rooms, under rococo cornices, drinking mean glasses of sweet wine, your heads bowed together, adopting the same low, regretful tone? Speaking together of 'Oscar, poor foolish, Oscar . . .'

Ross You made her promises. In prison you made her certain promises.

Wilde Well?

Ross These promises you have not fulfilled!

Wilde shakes his head, disbelieving.

Wilde What is this? Am I to be tried again? In my own living room? Is the universe now become a court of law? Were my three trials not enough? Were proceedings only temporarily suspended during my imprisonment? Are we now to put up the dark wood panelling and pull on our wigs again? What are we saying? Did rain stop play? Are we now to resume?

Ross Oscar, you made an agreement. You signed it.

Wilde So?

Ross She has the right to enforce it.

Wilde The right. What right? The same right she has to rebuke me? (*He stubs out his cigarette, furious.*) She charges me that I have not written to her. She sends me pictures of the children. I look at them. I cry. All evening I weep. What am I to say? How am I to write? She writes again. 'You have said nothing about the photos. What a brute you are! It is clear you do not love your children.' She wants me to answer. How can I? It is too cruel. I, who have spent my life holding language up to the light. Making words shimmer in the light. How am I to say to

84

her, 'I love my children so much I cannot write'? (*He is overwhelmed, on the verge of tears.*) It is all a bribe. It is all bribery. 'Behave as I would wish and one day you will see your children . . .' I sat with them, I played with them in the nursery. For years – yes, regardless – before the theatre, after the theatre – hurrying home to see my children – yes, even though I left to travel down the darkest East End street, to smear my mouth against men whose names I never knew, men whom I never saw, pressed against walls, in the dark, in the rough dark – yet every night I came home and told my children stories of ghosts, of fairies, of monsters and of enchanted lands . . . These are my children, Robbie. The nursery was my home, not the bedroom. (*He lifts one hand, helpless.*) And now she holds my boys like pieces in a game. She will move them forward or she will hold them back. It is not right. I have never seen them since the day I was sent to prison. What are we? Animals? Lower than animals. The animal holds its cub close, lets its cub come near . . . No, I cannot speak of it. (*He is too distraught to go on.*)

Ross Oscar, it is a war. You know that. She must use what she has. You must lay aside your feelings against her. They lead nowhere. They lead to your exclusion. They will lead to your extinction.

Wilde looks away, accepting what he says.

Wilde My life is spilt in the sand, red wine in the sand, and the sand drinks because it is thirsty and for no other reason. When will she stop and say 'Enough'?

Ross When you leave Bosie.

There is silence. The light has changed again, losing colour and warmth, chilly and very clear outside. It is dusk.

I am here today to tell you she will divorce you if you do not leave Bosie.

Wilde Leave him?

There is a pause.

Leave him? And go where?

Ross You promised not to take up with him. You signed a contract.

Wilde No.

Ross You did!

Wilde I have re-read the contract.

Ross Well, it is clear.

Wilde The contract which I signed while I was in prison specifies that I was not, on my release, to take up with a disreputable person.

Ross So? Well?

Wilde So. Lord Alfred Douglas is not a disreputable person.

Ross Oh, please!

Wilde He is not. Not legally. Not by legal definition. Because his reputation has not been tried. It has not been tried in a court of law.

Ross Are you serious? Are you seriously proposing this?

Wilde I am legally disreputable. But he is not. Oh yes, Bosie may not be liked. I have sensed sometimes that some of my friends do not like him. You yourself, Robbie, do not '*like*' him, am I right? I admit that I myself have used him to good effect in society. He serves as a repellant. He drives all kinds of unwelcome people away. It may be – I admit this also – that he is known throughout Europe as a gilded pillar of infamy. By rumour alone, he is a universal byword for sin and depravity. However. I have learnt something in my time in the courts. The fact is this: until he is tried he is not disreputable.

Ross You think this will help you? You think this argument will weigh?

Wilde Well, I am hoping it may.

Wilde smiles, skittish, but Ross is angry.

Ross Oscar, you know who he is. You know what he has done.

Wilde What exactly has he done?

Ross When you dismissed him, when in prison you said you would not see him again, when you finally told him that he was the cause of your downfall, what did he do?

Wilde Be quieter. He is above. He is in the room above.

Ross He tried to publish certain correspondence . . .

Wilde Do not speak of it!

Ross waits.

Do not speak of it! Do not go on!

Ross He intended to publish your letters. Why? To proclaim that you loved him, that he was the object of your love. He sought to publish proof, so that it could be *proved*, so that everyone would see, so it could not be denied. Why? For what reason? What was his reasoning? The most intimate things that had ever passed between you . . .

Wilde Do not say more!

Ross Endearments, pledges, declarations of feeling . . . to be bruited all over Europe, read in saloons and laughed at in gentlemen's clubs. To take the very heart of you and show it to the world . . . Do you think this was love? (*He stares at Wilde, demanding an answer.*) Well?

Wilde He panicked.

Ross Panicked?

Wilde Yes. He had not seen me. He was forbidden to see me.

Ross For good reason!

Wilde He was desperate. He thought publication would be helpful to our cause.

There is a pause. Wilde concedes.

All right, he lacks judgement.

Ross He lacks nothing. He is full of cunning.

Wilde is silent. Then looks away.

Wilde You know nothing of what passes between us.

Ross I know him well. He waited. It is clear. Your friends greeted you, your friends bought you a house, bought you a library. Installed you in the house. He waited. Your friends dined with you. They stayed with you. They left you alone to write. He waited. He waited until you were bored. Then he struck.

Wilde just looks at him, not answering.

Constance wrote to you. She asked you to visit her.

Wilde I could not visit her.

Ross Why not?

Wilde I was just out of prison. Be fair, Robbie. It was difficult. I was confused. I was not myself.

Ross Bosie asks, and you are back . . .

Wilde All right . . .

Ross . . . what? Within one week? Within ten days . . .

Wilde All right!

Ross Constance asks and you ignore her.

Wilde He offered me a place. Here we are. We would work together. We would write. It is a future.

Ross Do you wonder she is angry? The one thing she asks you not to do!

Wilde She? Not just she! The whole world! (*He laughs, bitterly.*) You are all spited. You are all rebuked. Every one of you. The world put me in prison in order to prove they could destroy my relationship with Lord Alfred Douglas.

Ross The world?

Wilde Yes. Now you discover you cannot. So the world seeks its revenge. (*He nods, sure of himself.*) I am shunned by you all, and my work goes unperformed, not because of the sin – never because of the sin – but because I refuse to accept the lesson *of* the sin. To alter my life now would be to admit I was wrong. A patriot put in prison for loving his country goes on loving his country. A poet in prison for loving boys loves boys. (*He looks at Ross unforgivingly.*) I have taken my punishment. Was that not enough? Was that not what was asked of me? Have I not suffered? Have I not endured? But no, the rules are now to be changed. I have done my term, but now new obligations are to be imposed. No longer is punishment enough. The moral *of* my punishment must be stuffed down my throat. I must choke on it.

He is so savage that Ross is stopped, hesitant to ask the next question.

Ross Do you really see no difference . . . Oscar, do you see no difference between those who put you in prison and those who now seek to help you?

Wilde Oh yes. There is a difference. Once I was punished from simple malice. Now I am punished in the interests of moral example.

Ross That is not fair.

Wilde Is it not? How do you see it then?

Ross is deeply shaken by Wilde's answer.

Please. Tell me. What, in fact, is my allowance? What am I paid? What does she pay me?

Ross Well . . .

Wilde Three pounds a week? Less. One-hundred-and-fifty pounds a year.

Ross Yes.

Wilde By a signed agreement. Signed by both parties.

Ross Exactly.

Wilde Negotiated by you. My only source of income. By divorcing me she discontinues that allowance. I am left with nothing.

Ross looks down.

Ross Yes.

Wilde The scheme now is that I shall have no food at all. It is proposed to leave me to die of starvation or to blow my brains out in a Naples urinal! And what's more, the scheme is put forward on moral grounds! What perfection of hypocrisy! (*He turns away, definitive now.*) Please, kill me because you hate me. But do not kill me because you wish to change me.

Ross Constance does not seek to kill you. You are doing it yourself.

Wilde waves a hand at him. Then, shaking, lights another cigarette.

Wilde Well, so be it. The public loves poets to die in this way. It seems to them poetically right.

Ross That may be the effect. Oscar, that is not the intention. Myself, I owe Constance nothing. She is not my friend. You are my friend. I have sought nothing but to go between you. Only to be the go-between.

Wilde Then get me some brandy.

The remark is brutal. The room is darkening. Wilde has not moved from his chair. Ross goes to pour from the bottle into Wilde's glass.

I have never come across anyone in whom the moral sense was dominant, who was not heartless, cruel, vindictive, log-stupid and entirely lacking in the smallest sense of humanity. Moral people are simple beasts. (*He looks at the measure Ross is pouring.*) Leave the bottle.

He is digging in for the evening. Ross puts the bottle down.

I have offered to live in separate quarters.

Ross That is not enough.

Wilde No?

Ross Be serious, Oscar.

Wilde I have offered to live two streets away.

Ross You know what she wants.

Wilde Do I? Do I, in fact? Two streets not enough? How many streets then? Three?

Ross shakes his head, despairing.

More? Would you bring us a globe then, Robbie? Shall
we sit, you and I, old friend, and look together at a map?
What distance are we talking of? Different towns?
Different countries? Different continents? Will you draw a
line which she considers just?

*Upstairs Galileo is heard, calling in Italian to Bosie.
Ross looks up as he pours himself another drink.*

Ross It is your business. It is your decision.

Wilde Yes. As you say.

Ross He is a repellant. Use him by all means. But repel-
lants are indiscriminate. They also drive away those
whom you will need as your friends.

*Bosie appears, dressed like an Englishman in pale
trousers and jacket, Galileo behind him. They are both
laughing, the picture of careless youth. Bosie has clearly
resolved to be easygoing to Ross.*

Bosie Ah, Robbie, greetings.

Ross Thank you.

Bosie You have made a long journey.

Ross Yes.

Bosie We have not seen you here before.

Ross No.

Bosie My friend Galileo is taking me out dancing. Do
you wish to accompany us?

Ross I cannot. I am leaving tonight. By the night train.

Bosie Already? (*He smiles affectionately at Wilde.*)
Oscar?

92

Wilde Forgive me. My dancing days are over. (*He reaches out to the table and holds up the letter between his fingers.*) Your mother's letter.

Bosie Thank you. (*He goes across the room to take it, perfectly at ease.*) Well, it was good to see you, Robbie. However briefly. Don't wait up. I'll be late.

Wilde You have your key?

Bosie I do. Goodbye, everyone. Enjoy yourselves.

Wilde Oh yes.

Galileo *Arrivederci. È stato un piacere. Alla prossima.*

Wilde Dance for me, Bosie. Dance one for me.

Bosie laughs and goes out with Galileo. Wilde reaches out and takes Ross's hand.

And will you not stay with me, Robbie? Will you not stay here tonight?

Ross I cannot.

Wilde No?

Ross Truly, I cannot. I must return to England.

Wilde Ah.

It is darkening now outside the window.

In prison, I tell you, after several months – I was ill, my stomach wrecked, attended by dysentery, working on a treadmill then thrown in my cell, gasping for breath, for air . . . the governor of the prison visited. He said, 'Wilde, you must learn patience . . .' I replied, 'Patience I would happily learn but what you are teaching me is apathy . . .'

Suddenly his eyes are filled with tears at the hopeless-

ness of his situation. Ross, kneeling before him, is also overwhelmed.

I have enjoyed our talk. I see no one. I shall miss you, Robbie. I shall miss the chance to talk.

Ross I am sorry. It hurts me to say . . . I do not know how to say this. But I must dispatch a message to Constance . . .

Wilde looks away, letting go of Ross's hand, not willing to dignify this with a reply. Ross knows the answer and gets up.

So. Well, it is so. Good to see you, Oscar. I have very little. I can leave you two pounds only. Even two pounds is not easy. My mother bought my ticket. I myself am at some considerable inconvenience. Yes, art is a thriving racket as you say, but not when you are known to be Oscar Wilde's oldest friend. (*He has the money in his hand.*) So? Shall I leave it here?

Wilde Leave it.

Wilde waves a finger like a cardinal. Ross puts the coins down on the table beside him. He wants to move close, but Wilde speaks to stop him.

I shall one day see you again.

Ross knows this is final. He goes, closing the door behind him. Wilde does not move. Music begins to play, swelling and filling the room. The light fades to near dark. The lighthouse beam sweeps round again from outside the window, catching Wilde briefly in the light.
There is a passage of time. It is night. Wilde is still sitting in the same chair. Most of the brandy has gone. Only his burning cigarette indicates his presence. Then light comes from a gaslamp held by Bosie as he comes

94

downstairs, still dressed. The music fades as Bosie is surprised to see Wilde. SCENE TWO.

Bosie Oscar . . .

Wilde turns slightly.

You're here.

Wilde Yes.

Bosie Were you here all along? Have you been sleeping?

Wilde No.

Bosie You did not hear me come in? Why did you not say anything? You did not speak to me.

Wilde I was struck dumb by the fact that you came back alone.

Bosie Very funny.

Wilde Thank you.

Bosie puts down his lamp and picks Wilde's notebook up from the table.

Bosie Ah, I see. Have you been writing?

Wilde Yes. I have been writing my play.

Bosie In the dark?

Bosie holds the book a moment, but Wilde takes it and puts it back down.

You are extraordinary.

Wilde You think so?

Bosie You sit here. When did you last move?

Wilde Oh, quite recently. I have occupied this chair for only one single transit of the sun.

Bosie lights another lamp and the room begins to brighten.

Do you know when I lived at Tite Street I once took a cab to a dinner party just three houses away?

Bosie Nothing surprises me.

Wilde It was my own individual protest against the mindless cult of athleticism.

Bosie smiles affectionately.

Buddhism, similarly, has always been a closed book to me. A whole religion devoted to the cause of breathing. To what purpose? We breathe anyway, will we, nill we. My own endeavour in breathing, as in all things, is to expend as little energy as possible.

Bosie Are you planning to move?

Wilde No.

Bosie Have you slept at all?

Wilde No.

It is the first time we have seen the two of them alone, and the tone is relaxed.

Ideally, I like to drink anise. My favourite anise is the second. I drink it not because it makes me sleep – nothing makes me sleep – but because at the moment I drink it I *believe* that I shall sleep. An illustration of the perfect usefulness of science. The potion necessary to make me sleep does not exist. But the potion that provides the illusion that I shall does.

Bosie Yes.

Wilde Indeed. (*He stubs out his cigarette.*) I drink the second anise. I am filled with the conviction 'I shall sleep tonight'. Belief is everything. Faith is everything. (*He is thoughtful a moment.*) It is the same with love.

Bosie With love?

Wilde Yes.

Bosie In what way?

Wilde The vulgar error is to think that love is a kind of illusion.

Bosie Is it not?

Wilde No. It is the fault of bad poets who encourage this mistake. 'I am completely enraptured,' lovers say, as if somehow they were being deceived. When the affair ends, they say, 'I have been stripped of my illusions.' When they cease to love, they say, 'Oh. I see him clearly now.'

Bosie Are they not right?

Wilde No, Bosie. The reverse is the truth.

The two men look at each other.

The everyday world is shrouded. We see it dimly. Only when we love do we see the true person. The truth of a person is only visible through love. Love is not the illusion. Life is.

There is a silence. Bosie shifts.

Bosie You heard me come in?

Wilde Yes, of course. Hours ago.

Bosie I was early.

Wilde I heard you moving about.

Bosie I have been thinking.

Wilde I can tell.

Bosie After all, we have been here three months.

Wilde Yes.

Bosie We cannot just go on.

Wilde No.

Bosie I mean, without money.

Wilde Plainly. As you say. You are right. *The Ballad of Reading Gaol* is to be published next year. A shamelessly commercial work. More low comedy. This time on the subject of prison reform. A heady profit of five pennies per copy is guaranteed.

Bosie What did Robbie say of it?

Wilde He did not mention it. My feeling is he did not like it. Silence is always the most potent form of literary criticism.

Bosie watches Wilde, wary now.

Bosie How was Robbie?

Wilde Robbie? Oh. Himself.

Bosie Yes. Robbie is always himself.

Wilde He is always quiet. People who speak quietly are always held to be modest. Why? It seems to me the height of arrogance not to make the effort to make yourself heard. Always I lean towards him. My ears are bad, but not that bad . . .

Bosie Yes.

Wilde Lord deliver us from the conceit of quiet speakers.

Bosie Did he bring you good news?

Wilde Good news?

Bosie A long way to come . . .

Wilde Indeed.

Bosie Can you tell me what he said?

  Wilde affects indifference.

Wilde He told me that Whistler is still at his daubs.

Bosie Oh . . .

Wilde The Café Royal is still full. Men sit taking care not to cross their legs. The wink is outlawed as an acceptable form of social intercourse. Gentlemen seeking advancement in society cover their arses with three layers of tailored material. Frankly, I should be carried shoulder-high by the cutters down Savile Row, for now a whole generation of respectable people must conceal their nether parts behind high-priced, redundant fabric. My arrest, thank God, has had some commercial benefits.

Bosie But not for you.

Wilde No. Surely. (*He knows he has not succeeded in sidetracking Bosie.*)

Bosie What do you propose?

Wilde Propose?

Bosie I am asking: what are you planning? Oscar, I have to insist: where are we headed?

  Wilde lights a cigarette, apparently to avoid answering.

Oscar, are you hiding something from me? Robbie must have come to some purpose. He must have come for some reason.

Wilde None.

Wilde throws him a quick glance, but Bosie is off now on a course of his own.

Bosie Oscar, I have come to a conclusion. That is why I was pacing.

Wilde Ah.

Bosie I have come to believe that we are in some way at fault.

Wilde At fault?

Bosie Has that not occurred to you?

Wilde frowns, not wanting to speak.

Do you think that human beings just live? The lot they are handed, the ordeals they undergo . . . do you think these depend purely on the workings of chance?

Wilde I am sorry. I am not following you.

Bosie looks at him, preparing himself.

Bosie Oscar, it is not my wish to hurt you . . .

Wilde Surely . . .

Bosie But do you not feel that the way we are living here in Naples – the place we find ourselves in – do you not find in this some sort of judgement?

Wilde Judgement?

Bosie Yes.

Wilde is frowning, bewildered.

Come. Look. Look around you. The empty rooms, the appalling lack of servants, the rats – please! The absence of money, the hunger even, the futility! You! I! Our ceaseless disputes! The sometimes barren evenings – has it not occurred to you, have you not thought? The nights, the nights you sit alone in that chair, the loss of your friends, the collapse of your reputation . . .

Wilde Ah, that.

Bosie starts to backtrack.

Bosie No . . .

Wilde Go on. Please. Build your case.

Bosie Oscar . . .

Wilde It is beginning to sound positively monumental.

Bosie smiles, apparently conceding.

Bosie I sound too harsh, it is not my wish to be unkind to you . . .

Wilde Never.

Bosie But have you never thought that perhaps we live like this because this is what we deserve?

Wilde Deserve?

Bosie Yes.

Wilde Goodness. A big word, 'deserve'. I have never been sure I understand it. Please. Explain to me gently. Possibly I am obtuse.

Bosie Oscar . . .

Wilde There is some justice, is that your contention?

Bosie Perhaps.

Wilde There is *justice*, is there? At work here we find our old friend, *fate*?

Bosie Well . . .

Wilde Fate is at work, is it? Doing its worst?

Bosie I fear so.

Wilde What you are suggesting is – let me be clear – you think that fate is not blind? What is this, Bosie? A late conversion?

Bosie No. An early conversion.

Wilde Fate has dealt us this hand, but only because – what? – we have lived in the wrong way?

Bosie Not we, Oscar. You.

Wilde nods, understanding at last.

Wilde Ah, I see. Yes of course. Now I have your drift. The old cause . . .

Bosie Yes . . .

Wilde The first source of our misfortunes. As you believe.

Bosie Not as I believe, Oscar. As it is.

Wilde nods.

Wilde Now I establish it. Now I am clear.

Bosie Yes.

Wilde We return. The *fons et origo*.

Bosie The decision to lie.

Wilde Oh, of course.

Bosie And the decision to persist in the lie. From this all else stems!

Bosie has suddenly raised his voice. Wilde reacts, reaching for the brandy.

Wilde I think I shall be needing a drink. We have discussed this, Bosie. We do not need to discuss it again. I think I preferred it when you spent the night fishing.

Bosie I cannot forgive you! I cannot forgive you this . . .

Wilde No, you have said.

Bosie Lying in public! Isn't that your principal achievement? Isn't that the thing for which you will be chiefly known?

Wilde It may be.

Bosie You were given your theatre! You were given your chance! The Old Bailey! You could have defended Greek love! (*He is passionate, indignant.*) How will history judge you? History will forget you . . .

Wilde No doubt.

Bosie You will be known for ever as the man who was ashamed to admit his own nature! Your plays will be forgotten. They will not be played. Why? Because you did not dare. Because you did not stand up.

Wilde You think that is the reason?

Bosie When a better time comes, when this kind of love is accepted and understood, then you will be condemned because you took the coward's way. (*He suddenly shouts out again.*) Did you ever consider the simple expedient of *telling the truth*?

Wilde In public?

Bosie Of course.

Wilde appears to think for a moment.

Wilde I think I can safely say never.

Bosie From this . . . from this central evasion, all else follows! With you, everything is compromise! Everything is dishonesty! I cannot live like this!

Wilde No, plainly.

Bosie is calmer, wanting to get to his real point.

Bosie Oscar, I have wanted to say for some time: it is worse, truly – I know this is difficult to hear – but, from my point of view, our situation is far worse for me.

Wilde Ah yes. (*He pauses a second.*) How so?

Bosie I am young.

Wilde Ah.

Bosie My life lies ahead of me.

Wilde Of course.

Bosie You are old. Your best days lie behind you.

Wilde I suppose. (*He looks mildly surprised.*) I mean, if you want to put it that way.

Bosie To be destroyed when you are in your forties, yes it is sad, yes it is tragic, of course. I do not deny it.

Wilde No . . .

Bosie I have never denied it. But for me! The prospect of being destroyed when my life is still before me!

Wilde Yes, I see. (*He flicks some ash, but Bosie is not listening.*) Plainly it's inconvenient.

Bosie I cannot allow it! (*He pauses, reaching the real subject.*) Also. Remember: we have not spoken much of this lately, but since I first met you, I have always told you, I have always made clear, it is not in my nature finally to be with men, to love men only . . .

Wilde No.

Bosie I am not disposed, as you are, to love my own sex . . .

Wilde is impassive, not responding.

For me, as you know, it has been only a phase . . .

Wilde Of course . . .

Bosie Since adolescence it is only a phase I have been passing through.

Wilde That's right. Though occasionally with an appetite which the imperceptive might mistake for positive relish.

Bosie nods as if this is just the kind of remark he had been expecting.

Bosie Oh yes, very good . . .

Wilde I'm sorry . . .

Bosie You may make your jokes . . .

Wilde Thank you.

Bosie You have always made cheap jokes.

Wilde No. Not always. Once people paid for them. And paid handsomely.

Bosie I am not an invert!

Wilde No.

Wilde pauses, then speaks quietly, but Bosie does not hear him.

Just a brilliant mimic.

Bosie Oh yes, certainly, as you say, I have indulged myself . . .

Wilde Yes. Once or twice . . .

Bosie I have had particular experiences. I have slept with men . . .

Wilde Now steady on, Bosie, don't get carried away . . .

Bosie I admit I have let events overtake me . . .

Wilde Indeed. That night in Capri.

Bosie Please! You have joked enough! (*He is momentarily threatening.*) I have indulged myself, yes, but always, *always* knowing that I could stop at any time.

Wilde That is fortunate.

Bosie At any time! (*He is relieved to have established his point.*) God knows, since I came down from Oxford, I have seen enough of your friends, I have known enough old queens . . .

Wilde Indeed.

Bosie My God! The horror of it. Ending up like that. No, thank you! To find myself at forty or fifty, painted, rouged, sitting in bars . . . no, not for me, that life. This is not the destiny of my family. That is not my future. I have always known that I would move on.

Wilde And will you? Is that what you are saying? Will you now move on?

There is the silence of a crucial point reached. Bosie is still, sincere.

Bosie Oscar, you know that I will not leave you. I will not leave you against your will. It would be wrong. I asked you here.

Wilde You did.

Bosie It was at my request. I shall not dishonour that request. Too many people have left you, too many people have betrayed you. You have not been good at choosing your friends.

Wilde On the contrary. I have the gift of choosing them. Holding on to them has proved to be my *faiblesse*.

Bosie Yes. You know what I mean.

Wilde I do.

There is a silence, each of them knowing what is coming. At the window, light is beginning to break, the first grey outline of morning on the horizon.

Dawn is coming. I know it. I shall not need to turn. Already I feel it like a hand. I feel the light at my back.

Bosie takes a step towards him.

Bosie Oscar . . .

Wilde You must forgive me, but I have heard you.

Bosie Heard me?

Wilde Yes.

Bosie What do you mean, you have heard me?

Wilde I have sat here. I have been listening. All night I have been listening. I have heard you moving overhead.

Bosie I see.

Wilde Every step, every movement you have made. I have heard your intent. I thought: a winter trip. Can it be? A return to Capri? But I reasoned that the season had ended. Even Europe's damned souls . . . even we do not go to Capri in December.

Bosie shifts uneasily.

Bosie Oscar, I had wanted to speak to you.

Wilde Ah. My fault again, is it?

Bosie No. I am not saying that. It is just . . . for you, yes, to be in Naples, to write every day . . . there is a project here for you which is virtuous, which makes sense. But for me there is nothing. Truly.

Wilde waits, saying nothing.

And I have a family to return to.

Wilde I see.

Sensing the quiet of Wilde's response, Bosie begins to gain in confidence.

Bosie My mother has written.

Wilde Yes. I had noticed that as well. I should request gainful employment as a concierge. I miss nothing. You have read the letter?

Bosie nods.

When did you read it?

Bosie Oh, at the café . . .

Wilde Ah . . .

Bosie With Galileo. That is when I decided to come back.

Wilde You were pleased with its contents, plainly?

Bosie She has offered me money.

Wilde Ah, good. Well, then . . .

Bosie She has offered me an allowance. She is willing to forgive. (*He looks down, moved.*) You must understand. For me, this is important.

Wilde Of course . . .

Bosie There are times – yes – when I have despaired even of my mother's love. I have not been certain she would love me again. But now she is prepared to overlook the past. (*He pauses before the crucial information.*) She is offering me three hundred pounds a year.

The two men look at one another.

Wilde Ah, well . . .

Bosie Yes . . .

Wilde Three hundred is something. No one can deny it. But tell me: this money, does it come with conditions?

Bosie Oscar . . .

Wilde What makes me ask this? Do I have gifts of the paranormal? Are there conditions attached?

Bosie looks at him, not answering.

After all, not one minute ago, you promised to stay with me.

Bosie I did.

Wilde So, then. I have sat here. I have listened. I have heard you upstairs. Are you the only man on earth who *packs his bags to stay where he is?*

Wilde has given these words sudden bite. In reply, Bosie becomes formal, as if summarizing a legal position.

Bosie You have heard me. Oscar, you have heard my intention. I have said I will not leave you without your consent. That is what I said. I await your consent.

Wilde says nothing. Bosie shakes his head slightly, as if injured by his silence.

I have wanted nothing but your happiness. I have wanted only to make you happy. But in this as in everything our relationship has been a failure. The habit of dishonesty goes deep in you.

Wilde Really?

Bosie suddenly raises his voice.

Bosie Why did you not speak? Why do you refuse to speak out?

Wilde I do not seek society's approval. I seek no one's approval. I live by my own lights and no one else's. There it is. There it ends.

Bosie How do you know? How do you know until you try?

The light is beginning to grow behind Wilde, taking on colour.

Wilde I appealed once in my life to the court of public opinion. And it gave society the chance it had been waiting for. Under no circumstances will I expose myself once more. If the cost of being understood is that I must issue manifestos, issue statements, hack out dull, fatuous slices of prose, full of abstract nouns, nouns as heavy as lead weights, then, no! The price is too high.

Bosie *Why?*

Wilde looks, the question self-evidently ridiculous.

Wilde Letters to papers? Tracts? Circulars eliciting support from the eminent in the sciences and the arts? Laborious explanations of the origins of a malady which is not a malady? Of a crime which is not a crime? To set my pen to paper even is to begin to confess. And, Bosie, I have nothing to confess! Even to ask, even to plead my case is to admit their right to judge me. I will not admit their authority. I will not plead. The work is there. The work is done. Now I ask no special favours. At no point have I complained. Please. Throw me off a cliff, or put me in a burning pit, but do not ask me to beg. Never ask me to beg.

Bosie is frowning, at an apparent impasse.

Bosie So what will you do? Will you live . . . will you go on living here alone?

Wilde I plan to live with you.

Bosie Oscar, I have said. It cannot be. I cannot live with you.

Wilde is smiling, infuriatingly calm.

Wilde Last night Robbie was sent here by my blackmailing wife. I refused to disown you. In return she has cut me off.

Bosie No!

Wilde Yes. Now I have nothing. It amuses me. I admit I am amused. How often have I said the words 'I cannot live without you'? Up till now, I have spoken them from the heart. Now I speak them from the pocketbook. Look in my eyes, Bosie. (*He looks up into Bosie's eyes.*) 'I cannot live without you.'

There is something so ridiculous in this that both men smile.

Bosie It is funny . . .

Wilde Yes.

Bosie In some way it is funny. (*He moves away, nodding.*) As it happens, I may be able to help you.

Wilde How?

Bosie You dislike my family, you think them inconsiderate. But you do not realize: they have long accepted some blame. They know that in bringing your prosecution you acted in some sense on my behalf.

Wilde In some sense?

Bosie Indeed. My family has known . . . the Queensberrys have known that they do have obligations towards you. There is a debt of honour. My mother says in her letter that she wishes to make that debt concrete.

Wilde Concrete?

Bosie In her letter she says this.

Both men are now tense, Wilde poker-faced, knowing the end is near.

Wilde Ah, well.

Bosie Yes . . .

Wilde To the heart of things.

Bosie Yes.

Wilde Just how much concrete is she offering?

Bosie is ready, precise.

Bosie She will pay you two hundred.

Wilde Two?

Bosie In two instalments.

Wilde When?

Bosie The first at once.

Wilde A hundred at once?

Bosie Yes.

Wilde The second?

Bosie Within a month.

Wilde Two? Is that all?

Bosie No. (*He pauses slightly.*) Three hundred more as soon as she has it.

Wilde Five? Five in all? Five hundred?

Bosie nods. Wilde is impassive.

Bosie She attaches one condition. To your money, as to my own.

Wilde Of course. The whole world wants that condition. Here we are, hurting no one. And yet.

The light is growing behind Wilde. He tries to stir. His limbs are stiff.

I have sat here too long. I need to move. Help me.

Bosie goes over and takes both Wilde's hands. Agonizingly, he pulls Wilde's bent figure to his feet. Wilde pulls himself upright. He looks around and then takes a few shaky, wheezing steps.

Thus it is. It is done.

Bosie You agree?

Wilde How can I not agree? More conventionally it is you who should receive the pieces of silver, but in this case it is me. (*He waves a hand.*) You are free. You have always been free. Go.

Wilde goes out. Bosie looks at the room for the last time. Wilde comes back surprisingly soon, and surprisingly quickly, carrying a glass of water.

No speeches, please, Bosie. No reproaches. I have a horror of sentimentality. The lump in my throat is not from the release of my emotions but from the tightening of the noose. (*He looks casually at Bosie.*) When is your train?

Bosie Soon.

Wilde The first train?

Bosie Yes. It leaves very soon.

Wilde And the first hundred? When will I see that?

He has moved to another chair from which he can watch the dawn. The speed of his acceptance has made Bosie uncomfortable.

Bosie Oscar, I can say I feel often like an actor who has been cast in the wrong part. I was never born to be a rebel . . .

Wilde No.

Bosie I met you purely by accident. And yet I often consider how because of that accident I have become an outcast.

Wilde Indeed.

Bosie To me this is a paradox. All I have ever wanted is reconciliation with my family. This way I have it.

Wilde Well, then. You are fortunate.

Bosie In my mother's offer I see some way back.

Wilde Good. No doubt you will achieve what you wish. In your layer of society, ties of blood always triumph over ties of sentiment. I will be happy to be the agent of the Queensberry family reunion. Plainly if the Queensberrys are reunited, then my passage of suffering has not been in vain.

Bosie can hardly miss his tone.

Bosie Oscar, I would not wish you bitter.

Wilde No? Not bitter, then. How would you wish me?

Bosie Oscar, we have tried. We have truly tried.

Wilde Oh yes.

Bosie I am fond of you. At the end, I would wish you at peace.

Wilde smiles, amused by this remark.

Wilde At peace? Oh, surely. Do not fear for me. I have understood my actions, as you have not yet understood your own.

Bosie What do you mean?

Wilde The governing principle of my life has been love. But of yours, it has been power.

Bosie looks at him, horrified.

It is the family failing. I am sorry for you, Bosie. A love of power confers a whole bouquet of rewards, but peace is not among them.

Bosie is silent.

You called me back, you led me to Naples, not as an expression of your feelings, but in a demonstration of your will.

Bosie That is not true.

Wilde Do not distress yourself. I promise you, I shall be at my peace long before you are.

He says this oddly. Bosie is disturbed.

Bosie What are you saying?

Wilde You have taken from me the thing you most envied.

Bosie What is it?

Wilde What you have wanted all along.

He puts his glass down, and goes back to his old seat. He picks up his notebook and holds its blank pages up in the air. Bosie looks across at the empty book above Wilde's head.

There is nothing. The pages are empty. What do I write?

Shopping lists for things I have no money to buy. You have achieved your aim. You have achieved my silence.

Bosie is outraged at the accusation.

Bosie How can you say that? How can you say such a thing? I respect your talent. I revere it. I am a poet myself!

Wilde smiles to himself but Bosie moves round the room in genuine shock.

What, you would leave me thus? With this accusation? You would accuse me – what? – of wanting to silence the greatest dramatist of the modern stage?

Wilde Are you the excuse for my silence? Or the cause of it? Whichever, that is the effect. That is the result. To lose my life will be as nothing. But to lose my art . . . (*He is calm, as if the moment of Bosie's departure has conferred an odd confidence on him.*) Come towards me. Walk. Take some steps. Our business is not complete.

Bosie moves slowly towards him.

I have known you six years. I will know you no longer. Come closer.

They are now unnaturally close, just short of touching.

You will never be free until you ask my forgiveness. Kiss me.

And Bosie leans in for the Judas kiss. It is quite short, and when it is over Wilde smiles almost contentedly, a rite enacted. He puts a hand kindly on Bosie's arm.

And now I imagine you must go on your way.

Bosie turns and goes out. The sun is coming up, beginning to give warmth to the room. Wilde turns out the lamps, then drinks the remains of his water. On the

*stairs Bosie reappears, carrying his luggage. He puts it
down by the door.*

In prison I had the chance to read the Christ story. Over
and over. It seemed to me the greatest story I ever read.
But it has one flaw. Christ is betrayed by Judas, who is
almost a stranger. Judas is a man he doesn't know well. It
would be artistically truer if he were betrayed by John.
Because John is the man he loves most.

*This has been said without bitterness or accusation.
And Bosie does not seem offended, just at the end of a
chapter.*

I shall not live long. The English will not allow themselves
to enter another century with me still alive.

Bosie nods slightly.

Bosie Well, I should be going then.

Wilde Yes.

Bosie It's time I was leaving. If there are any letters, will
you send them on?

Wilde I shall.

Bosie So.

There is a moment's pause.

Goodbye then, Oscar.

Wilde Goodbye.

*Bosie goes out. Wilde opens the balcony doors to catch
the warmth of the morning sun. The music plays.
Although Wilde is turned away, his voice fills the theatre.*

All trials are trials for one's life, just as all sentences are
sentences of death, and three times I have been tried. The
first time I left the box to be arrested, the second time to

be led back to the House of Detention, the third time to pass into a prison for two years. Society, as we have constituted it, will have no place for me, has none to offer; but Nature, whose sweet rains fall on unjust and just alike, will have clefts in the rocks where I may hide, and secret valleys in whose silence I may weep undisturbed. She will hang the night with stars so that I may walk abroad in the darkness without stumbling, and send the wind over my footprints so that none may track me to my hurt: she will cleanse me in great waters, and with bitter herbs make me whole . . .

Wilde goes back to his chair where he picks up his book and starts to read. The sun rises, brilliant now over the sea.